TOURISM WRITING

TOURISM WRITING

A New Literary Genre
Unveiling the History, Mystery, and Economy of Places and Events

Christmas 2018
To Kathy Russell,
Thanks for reading my book,
Best regards,

Mary S. Palmer

Mary S. Palmer

Universal-Publishers
Irvine • Boca Raton

Tourism Writing: A New Literary Genre Unveiling the History, Mystery, and Economy of Places and Events

Copyright © 2018 Mary S. Palmer. All rights reserved.
No part of this publication may be reproduced, distributed, or transmitted in any form or by any means, including photocopying, recording, or other electronic or mechanical methods, without the prior written permission of the publisher, except in the case of brief quotations embodied in critical reviews and certain other noncommercial uses permitted by copyright law.

Universal Publishers, Inc.
Irvine • Boca Raton
USA • 2018
www.universal-publishers.com
2018

ISBN: 9781627342490 (pbk.)
ISBN: 9781627342506 (ebk.)

Typeset by Medlar Publishing Solutions Pvt Ltd, India
Cover design by Ivan Popov

Publisher's Cataloging-in-Publication Data

Names: Palmer, Mary S., author.
Title: Tourism writing: a new literary genre unveiling the history, mystery, and economy of places and events / Mary S. Palmer.
Description: Irvine, CA : Universal Publishers, 2018.
Identifiers: LCCN 2018938750 | ISBN 978-1-62734-249-0 (pbk.) | ISBN 978-1-62734-250-6 (ebook)
Subjects: LCSH: Travel writing. | Tourism--Economic aspects. | Tourism--Marketing. | Authorship. | BISAC: LANGUAGE ARTS & DISCIPLINES / Authorship. | BUSINESS & ECONOMICS / Industries / Hospitality, Travel & Tourism.
Classification: LCC PN56.T7 P35 2018 (print) | LCC PN56.T7 P35 2018 (ebook) | DDC 809/.93355--dc23.

DEDICATION

*To all who helped me along the way
on my own literary journey*

TABLE OF CONTENTS

Author's note: Although the examples used in this book refer to Alabama and surrounding states, similar types of less known unique places and events exist in all fifty of the United States, waiting to be sought out and revealed to readers. To appeal to all types of bibliophiles, instead of a didactic recitation, interviews and short stories illustrate why Tourism Writing is vitally important.

Dedication v
Foreword by Congressman Jo Bonner ix
Acknowledgements xi
A Note from the Director of Faulkner University:
Mobile Campus xiii
Introduction by Patrick Miller xv
    Why xv
    Wherefore xxi

1   A Full Life 1
2   Schools 5
3   Students 19
4   Teachers 23
5   Business 31

6	Tourism	49
7	Restaurants	55
8	History	65
9	Parks	69
10	Traveling Academics: Advanced Form of Travel Tourism Writing by Paula Webb	75
11	Politicians	85
12	Real Estate	91
13	Cemeteries	95
14	Police	101
15	Military	105
16	Museums	109
17	Unusual Influences	117
18	Hotels, and Bed and Breakfasts	129
19	Bicentennial	133
20	Entertainment	135
21	Homeless	147
22	Farming	151
23	Nashville	155
24	Congressional Record	163
25	Write Right and Share Attractions to Encourage Tourists	169
	Afterword	*179*
	Bibliography	*181*
	About the Author	*187*

FOREWORD

by Congressman Jo Bonner

Once again, one of Mobile's most gifted authors has been tasked with the ultimate challenge, penning *Tourism Writing: A New Literary Genre Unveiling the History, Mystery, and Economy of Places and Events* in time for the celebration of Alabama's Bicentennial birthday in 2019.

When I was afforded the high honor of representing my home state in the U.S. Congress, I had the pleasure of co-chairing the bipartisan Congressional Travel & Tourism Caucus with my good friend, Representative Sam Farr, a Democrat from California.

Sam and I rarely saw eye-to-eye on most of the political battles of the day. But we were in complete agreement when it came to raising public awareness about the economic importance of travel and tourism, whether in his beachside cities on the Pacific Coast or on my more remote coastal communities along the beautiful Gulf of Mexico.

If you don't think tourism and travel are big business, just check out the number of travel magazines and books next time you are at the grocery store, local library or bookstore. The reason there are so many publications is because travel and tourism are really big business.

For instance, domestic and international travelers generated $2.1 trillion in economic output in 2013, supporting a total of 14.9 million American jobs. The travel sector is also America's largest service export, fueling one in every nine U.S. jobs.

Therefore, it only makes sense that tourism literature is a vitally important way of introducing the reader to the splendors of a community; the really good writers are able to use their pen and paper to paint an inviting portrait of a place one must visit.

No one is better qualified to spark the imagination and talents of a whole new generation of future authors than Mary Palmer. Her book, *Tourism Writing: A New Literary Genre Unveiling the History, Mystery, and Economy of Places and Events* may well become the spark plug needed for an entirely new generation of writers. As they say, buckle up and have fun on the journey!

Jo Bonner
U.S. Congressman (2003–2013)

ACKNOWLEDGEMENTS

This book was written with a Faulkner University Grant. Many thanks to Dr. James Guy and to all involved in the process of awarding the grant that made this book possible.

A special thanks to Congressman Jo Bonner, who wrote the Foreword illustrating the importance of Tourism Writing, to Patrick Miller and Paula Webb, who added flavor to this book by contributing chapters in the areas of their expertise, and to Mrs. Diane Newell for her informative note.

Additional gratitude is due to all who invested their time to help complete this project. The contributions of the people listed were invaluable: Congressman Bradley Byrne, David Clark, Tighe Marston, Wes Smith, Wendy James, Bill James, Charlette Solis, Shannon Brown, Tish Williams, George Williams, Myrna Green, Councilman Fred Richardson, Brian Norris, Margaret Powers, Meg McFayden, Jason Wright, Judy Sigler, Powell Hamlin, Police Chief Lawrence Battiste, Executive Director of Public Safety

James Barber, Beth Armfield, Scott Tindle, Mike Bunn, Ann Pond, Ph.D, David Montiel, Md., Philip Levin, Md., Judge Jim Fraiser, Hill Goodspeed, Daryn Glassbrook, Ron Lambert, Ben Davis, Chuck Beard, Harry Palmer, Marcia Cornett, Charles Cornett, Benny Berlin, Denis Palmer, Sheila Palmer, Lieutenant Colonel John Schluter, USAF (Retired), Jack Schluter, Judith Jacob, NFG USAF (Retired) Michael Palmer, Steve Palmer, Stacey Cornett, Grady Earnheart, Bill Sparkman, Joyce Bowers, Neal Allison, James Guy, Ph.D, Breanna Yarborough, Kyle Morris, Arnie Cink, Nolan White, Brian Jones, Vinson Bradley, John Woods, Gavin Schneider, Chuck Torry, Bob Kirby, Margaret Daniels, Donna Baker, Ph.D, Chae Levy, Eva Golson, Sonny McCoy, Professor James Day, Karen Peterson, Jason McKenzie, Dr. John Borom, and Ashley Flowers.

A NOTE FROM THE DIRECTOR OF FAULKNER UNIVERSITY: MOBILE CAMPUS

Dear Readers:

Recently, as I unlocked my office and entered, I noticed someone had slipped a paper under the door. It was a note from a student. He wanted to explain the reason that he walked out of one of his classes. He stated, "I was bored…." Although that may not have been justifiable it shows that students today need more than facts; they need adventure. Tourism Writing can fulfill that need and make education come alive.

    Education is more than sitting in a classroom listening to a lecture or reading a textbook. Educating oneself can be discovered through the eyes of an adventurous tourist. This is true whether you choose to step out of your back door and enter into a world of knowledge about your local area, or opt to travel long distances seeking educational adventures.

Teaching students how tourism affects our economy and how it impacts our environment can help develop a higher level of understanding and possibly a desire to become involved. One of the assignments I gave my students was to pick a local event or attraction in our area and write a persuasive speech about it. The assignment became a great tool to promote tourism. Several of the students went to the attraction or event to learn more about it and came back with a new appreciation for our local area.

Years ago, a friend, whose husband's job required them to move frequently, told me that when they relocated to a new place she considered it a vacation. She took advantage of the opportunity to explore the area and visit as many of its interesting sites as possible. She commented that it surprised her how many people who had lived in that area most of their lives had not visited local tourist attractions.

As Nelson Mandela rightly noted, "Education is the powerful weapon which you can use to change the world (OBI CHINEDU BASIL, University of Calabar, Nigeria, FTMS Magazine, Maiden Edition). Education is the powerful weapon with which tourism development and sustainability can be achieved. Adding Tourism Writing to college courses can provide students with that weapon.

Diane Newell

INTRODUCTION

by Patrick Miller

WHY

The first question people usually ask me about the Southeastern Literary Tourism Initiative—SELTI for short—is how it all got started. The idea first crystalized after I entered one of my short stories into a competition for Southern gothic fiction in 2008. The inspiration for the story's setting had come many years earlier when I was fifteen and a friend and I had taken a short road trip to Cahawba, the ruins of Alabama's first state capital from 1820. The bustling river town had been abandoned in the latter part of the nineteenth century, leaving behind a mysterious place between the confluences of two beautiful rivers. We were fascinated by the powerful and sad inscriptions on the antebellum gravestones. One still stands out strongly in my memory: the message on a seventeen year-old's headstone: *Everything Bright Must Fade*. How could her grieving parents have known on the day of her burial that one day the town itself would become the neglected tombstone of a long-forgotten dream? There were stories to tell in this place, but many of those stories were lost forever.

One way to bring them back was through the vehicle of fiction. Many years later, when I learned about the Southern gothic writing contest, I wrote the short story inspired by Cahawba called "The Last Confession." The story was accepted as one of ten that were included in the anthology *Southern Gothic Shorts* by PJM Publishing. I thought other readers might enjoy visiting the place that inspired the story, so I asked the publisher if he wanted to include an article about Cahawba on his website in connection with the anthology. He loved the idea, and we put it together, me writing the content and him producing the graphics for the article. I wrote a press release about the project, and two state newspapers ran a feature about how the fictional story could generate tourism to the real setting through the online article and web links.

Those newspaper articles were the first media attention my fiction received, and naturally I was pleased with the result. However, I kept wondering: wouldn't it be great if there were a website that featured lots of different fictional stories written by lots of different authors about lots of different places to visit? After all, if the idea of directly linking fiction to tourism is good in Alabama, wouldn't it also be good in Mississippi, Georgia, Tennessee, Florida, the Carolinas, and all the other Southern states? And if writers did produce stories like that all over the South, wouldn't it be better if they were all linked together rather than being many different unconnected projects?

I researched whether a website or project like that existed and quickly found that it did not. The closest project was the Southern Literary Trail, but that was limited to classic twentieth century writers like Faulkner, Fitzgerald, and Harper Lee. What about something for twenty-first century writers?

The more I thought about the idea of tourism fiction, the more it all made sense. Readers would enjoy stories set in places they could visit verses places that didn't exist. If they visited the places, then they would talk about them more to their friends and family, which would sell more books. Selling more books would generate more profits for publishers, more commissions for agents, and more royalties for authors. Cities that were featured in stories would bring in more tourism dollars, which would mean more consumer spending in local hotels, restaurants, and retail shops on top of whatever attractions were visited. All that extra spending would also generate more tax revenue and jobs.

States and cities often spend huge sums of money trying to attract conventions for the tourism revenue. Why not spend a smaller portion of that amount on trying to attract fiction writers to feature their area's best attractions? Places like Cahawba were already ideal places for a story, so that would be an easy sell. All the writers had to do was set their stories in places that were really interesting and then, at the end, invite readers to visit. The cities and states that they wrote about would help publicize the books in ways that traditional fiction books never benefitted from. After all, what writer or publisher wouldn't want to benefit from the powerful marketing engines of a state and city tourism agency to help create buzz about a new book? And what state or city wouldn't want a commercial fiction writer to invite their readers to come visit their best tourism attractions that were just featured in a new novel or anthology? Given the choice between setting a novel in a real place and garnering that kind of extra publicity or setting a novel in a fictional or nondescript place and fighting it out in the competitive fiction market, most writers would choose the extra publicity.

The problem was that no cities or states were offering that extra publicity yet. No publishers or literary agents were asking for tourism manuscripts. In bookstores and Amazon, there were nonfiction travel sections but no "fiction travel" sections where all the novels were set in real places. There were no social media groups or chat rooms where readers conversed about their favorite tourism novels and even made plans for group tours. There were no bestseller lists for tourism novels because there were no tourism novels to be on a list yet. There were no financial incentives or grants for tourism fiction being offered by cities or states. There were no tourism fiction classes or writing programs being taught in college English classes, much less English degrees with a tourism fiction focus.

At the same time that none of this was happening, the publishing industry was going through painful upheaval by the arrival of tablet readers like the Kindle and Nook, both of which had the capability to embed tourism website links directly into a novel or short story anthology (although that wasn't happening because there were no tourism novels yet). Also at the same time, the tourism industry was going through the painful upheaval of the Great Recession, where potential tourists were less likely to spend more money on travel. Cities and states that relied on tourism dollars for desperately needed revenue were slashing budgets and payrolls for important public services to try and survive the difficult economic climate.

My thought was that both the publishing and tourism industries could strengthen each other by becoming partners along with public tourism agencies and visitor bureaus. After all, if a tourism novel were to bring in an extra one thousand tourists, then that would be the equivalent of a convention of a thousand people. What if a tourism novel brought in an extra one-hundred-thousand tourists? That would be the equivalent of one hundred conventions of a thousand people each! What city wouldn't want to benefit from that ramped up level of extra tourism dollars?

As I stated, however, none of the publicity or market infrastructure was in place yet to do any of this. Everything had to start somewhere. I had entered a contest and gotten my short story published in an anthology. The story had been featured in the media locally. What was the next step?

I did what many people were doing at the time: I started a blog. Although I had never used HTML code before, the new services made operating with it very user-friendly, much like computers themselves had become much more user friendly than in the eighties. I determined that every feature on the blog would include fiction or poetry set in real place. Each feature would also highlight the place with photos, links for readers to learn more, and especially a direct invitation for readers to come visit the place.

The first story published on the blog was "The Last Confession" with a longer online tourism guide than the one from the original contest. However, I quickly sought out other writers to contribute. Soon, a poet from Tupelo named Patricia Neely-Dorsey contacted me about publishing an excerpt on SELTI from her Mississippi-inspired poetry book. I had a great deal of fun working to complete that project with her, and we are still friends. She loved the tourism connection and her work has now earned her status as an official Goodwill Ambassador for the State of Mississippi.

I started seeking out published novels set in real places around the South and producing online tourism photo-features for them on SELTI, with links to the places and to the stores that sold the books. All of the features are still available online in the SELTI archives at http://southeasternliterarytourisminitiative.blogspot.com/.

One of the things I loved about novels was that they could introduce readers to multiple places rather than the one or two in a short story. None of the novels I profiled first on SELTI directly invited readers to visit the places or provided them with links at the end; the SELTI features were done after the book was published, so it was too late to add a tourism guide like that inside the novels themselves. Being intrigued by the new tablet readers and their Internet capabilities, I published my novel *Blind Fate,* set in Montgomery, on Kindle and included all the tourism links at the end with a brief tourism guide. Since no other novels had done that yet with a tourism focus, *USA Today* featured the novel in an October 2011 article. The *USA Today* article caught the attention of the Alabama Tourism Department, which plugged the article into their tourism newsletter. The development director of the University of Alabama Museums read the article from the state newsletter and contacted me about doing a project with her institution. And so began SELTI's—and the nation's—first tourism fiction contest, which would open up a whole new chapter in SELTI's future.

Mission Statement: SELTI seeks to enhance the public reading experience while improving local economies by encouraging writers to compose works of tourism literature. Tourism literature is inspired by real locations and also includes an invitation and guide showing readers how to visit the settings.

WHEREFORE

I arrived at Moundville Archaeological Park in November of 2011 to meet Kelli Harris, the Development Director for the University of Alabama Museums, and Dr. Bill Bomar, Executive Director of Moundville Archaeological Park. Moundville had once been the capital city of a Native American river empire but was found abandoned by the earliest European explorer who found only large empty mounds. To this day, no one knows for sure why Moundville was abandoned by the Native Americans about five hundred years ago: the perfect mystery for fiction writers to try and solve.

As I gazed at the haunting mounds just inside the park's entrance gates, I felt the power of the place creeping into my soul and my imagination. If I were writing a fictional story about this place, I would have the tale begin with some archaeologists discovering something very intriguing—but what? Rather than write the story myself, I thought it would be interesting to open the challenge up to many writers and see what they came up with. I proposed a short story contest on this concept to Kelli and Bill, who agreed the idea was worth trying, especially since Moundville was connected officially to the nearby University of Alabama, a wealth of talent. The contest would be open to the public, free to enter, and require writers to compose short stories set in Moundville. The winning story would be published online at SELTI and include a short tourism guide with photos and links like the other features. Three University of Alabama English professors would judge the entries.

Like many Alabama natives, I had visited Moundville on a field trip during grade school. Since then, Kelli and Bill had overseen a multi-million dollar capital campaign for the park which resulted in renovating the old 1930's building into a stunning new museum exhibit. Also, each October, a large Native American festival was held at Moundville with thousands of tourists and exhibitions of authentic Native American crafts and culture. All of this sounded perfect for the contest project. I was excited to experience the unleashing of creative writing applied to a specific tourism attraction like Moundville. The local newspaper, the *Tuscaloosa News*, helped to publicize the contest through an article.

Once the entries came in, I was amazed at the level of writing and how well it fit the purpose of promoting Moundville and bringing it alive through fiction. The stories were beautiful, powerful, and even evocative. However, one story's concept jumped out with genius. A woman named Kathryn Lang opened her story with two archaeologists discovering the body of a white female buried in the mound—the victim of a murder from only twenty years before. Two investigators were trying to figure out who the victim was and how she ended up buried in a mound that should have only held the remains of Native Americans from centuries—not decades—before. I would have never thought of that idea on my own, and it showed me the value of opening up these challenges to see what writers would create.

I wanted to shower publicity on Kathryn and the contest, so I developed the first SELTI Tourism Fiction Award, to be presented to Kathryn at the October Moundville Native American Festival. The presenter was Kathryn's state senator Clay Scofield, who also served on the state's Tourism and Marketing Committee. On the day of the award, a reporter named Stan Ingold from Alabama Public Radio came out to interview all of us, including myself, Kathryn, Dr. Bomar, and Senator Scofield. The interview is still available on APR's archives online. Senator Scofield used his speech at the festival to ask all writers to consider promoting unique Alabama attractions through their fiction. This was the first time any politician in the nation had called for something like that and was an important first step.

Like the *USA Today* article, the radio interview caught the attention of someone else who wanted to participate in a SELTI project. Olivia Grider, who was starting a lifestyle magazine with her husband Randy featuring the Lookout Mountain area in northeast Alabama, heard the interview. She contacted me and asked if SELTI could cosponsor the next contest with their magazine, *Lookout Alabama*. Perfect timing for all of us. The winner of the Lookout Alabama contest would not only have their story published online at SELTI but also in the Grider's beautiful new print magazine. In addition, the Alabama Tourism Department offered to sponsor a first place prize of $500. The two county tourism councils helped the magazine spread the word about the contest to the local community and through the media. The magazine got New York Times bestselling author Homer Hickam to help judge the contest, which helped gain more media exposure.

The winner of the contest, Natalie Cone, wrote a touching story featuring the scenic setting of Desoto State Park. She had also included as one her real settings a real bookstore and clerk in downtown Fort Payne, which was a wonderful touch. The magazine was launched in the spring of 2013 at Cook's Castle, a storybook location on its own that could have inspired a story. Senator Scofield presented the second SELTI Tourism Fiction Award to Natalie, this time with a check from the state tourism department.

There were five finalists in the Lookout Mountain SELTI contest. The finalists' stories were so good that the Griders published all of their stories in separate monthly editions of their magazine. Moving forward, I found that reading several stories about the same area provided a deeper understanding of the area than just one story, a development that would prove true in every contest.

The third contest featured the Mobile Bay area, which included cities like those across the bay, such as Fairhope. The Baldwin and Mobile County governments helped to promote the contest to the media and community. Once again, the range of stories showed the many layers of tourism attractions in the area. The winning story was written by Mary Palmer, a local college English instructor who composed a story highlighting the family-friendly nature of Mobile's Mardi Gras parades. This time, the SELTI Tourism Fiction Award was presented by the local congressman, Bradley Byrne, at the colorful Mobile Mardi Gras Museum. Congressman Byrne also gave a short speech on the floor of Congress honoring Mary's story and inviting others in the nation to consider how the idea of tourism fiction could benefit their districts as well.

After the contest, another local English professor began challenging her students to compose works of tourism literature, which I then published online at SELTI. This was the first time this type of writing had been assigned and taught in a college class, another important beginning for the future genre. After all, what if someday every college English creative writing program in the country were training future writers how to promote tourism attractions in their fiction? What would be the ultimate impact of that on the tourism and publishing industries as some of those writers went on become national and worldwide bestsellers? We were taking the first steps in tourism fiction through SELTI, but the concept of tourism fiction would grow far beyond us once it caught on. In order for that to happen, it had to start somewhere.

By the time of the Mobile SELTI contest, Kathryn Lang had joined the SELTI team and gave a talk to the crowd at the award presentation. Natalie Cone, a former SELTI contest winner, was one of the judges of the contest. I was staying in touch with each winner, and eventually, that would help with the formal organization of SELTI as a nonprofit instead of a blog. When it came time to nominate board members for SELTI, Kathryn and Mary Palmer were obvious choices.

The fourth SELTI contest featured the Huntsville area, home to the U.S. Space and Rocket Center. I was sure Huntsville's high-tech culture would produce a winning story that highlighted the future, but it was actually a haunting tale about Huntsville's distant past that won the contest. Natalie Cone's short story "Haunted Identity" won, but the city judges had no idea who she was until after they had voted for her. I liked judging that was blind to any aspect other than writing talent. Natalie's story wound together Huntsville's historic district in a unique and ultimately touching way that defines so much of her writing. She was presented with the 2015 SELTI Tourism Fiction Award and $500 prize at the Inaugural Rocket City Lit Fest, a gathering of many local writers, publishers, and readers.

The fifth SELTI contest focused on one of Alabama's—and the South's—most important historical towns: Selma. In 1965, a large group of Civil Rights protestors were severely beaten while trying to cross the Edmund Pettus Bridge on the edge of Selma. Civil Rights protestors had been beaten before, but not so dramatically on national television by state troopers. The nation was horrified at the images, and the tragedy soon resulted in quick passage of the 1965 Civil Rights Act that forever changed our nation for the better. I knew that a powerful story would have to come out highlighting this seminal moment on the verge of history changing.

Like other times before in the SELTI contests, I was surprised again at where the creativity coalesced around a winning story. The first place story featured Kenan's Mill, the oldest operating water-powered mill in the state from the antebellum period. Even though I had travelled to the Selma area many times, even written about a place in the county, I had still never heard of this unique place, which also hosted an annual festival each year of historical crafts and music. To me, this was exactly what tourism fiction was about: introducing readers to a fascinating place that they would have never known about outside of the story. I couldn't wait to visit the real Kenan's Mill.

Congresswoman Terri Sewell, the local representative, presented the 2016 SELTI Tourism Fiction Award to Charisa Hagel, a recent graduate of Faulkner University in Montgomery. The photo that ran in the Selma Times Journal about Charisa showed her receiving the award from Congresswoman Sewell inside the mill that she had used as a setting for the story. This was fiction jumping off the page and into real life.

The Selma SELTI contest also demonstrated another important aspect of tourism fiction: it enjoyed strong bipartisan support. Congressman Byrne from Mobile was a staunch Republican conservative, and Congresswoman Sewell was a Democratic liberal, but both saw the practical potential for tourism writing in their districts. A couple of years before, the Alabama Legislature had passed a resolution unanimously supporting tourism fiction. The ground was fertile; it just had to be sowed with literary seeds to produce fruit. Local, state, and federal governments all supported the idea, the media was willing to publicize it whenever projects were implemented, and writers responded well. Even so, like anything in our world, the idea needed money and attention to move forward.

After several contests, I saw the need to establish more stable and substantial funding, so I began to research and organize a project to convert SELTI into an official nonprofit, a rather large task for a small entity. However, the future seems bright and full of hope for tourism fiction. If things work well in Alabama, then they will work even better in the larger South, then the nation, then who knows? With a little vision, we can say: then the world.

1
A FULL LIFE

Some people say all of life is about money, if you have enough of it you can have a full life. Is that true? Perhaps it depends on the definition of the words "full life." Money allows you to have luxuries only the rich can afford, without being restricted to simply having the basic needs of food, shelter and clothing. Wealthy people can feast on gourmet food, own a mansion full of servants, and wear designer clothing. Money also offers opportunities not available to those of lesser means, such as an education at an Ivy League school or inheriting a successful business. However, it doesn't provide anyone the intelligence to succeed at those schools or even the common sense to make logical business decisions to keep a company operating. And money certainly doesn't instill in anyone an appreciation of cultural things or a good sense of values. It takes exposure to both to spark an interest.

The Declaration of Independence states that all United States citizens have "the right to life, liberty and the pursuit of happiness," and that "all men are created equal." Those basic rights offer opportunities available to all. Nonetheless, it is up to each individual as to how he, or she, lives that life, uses that freedom, and pursues that happiness. We can survive with simple food, modest shelter, and plain clothing. We can also limit our education, or get loans and work our way through college.

Happiness is a different matter. Notice the phraseology. We're not insured happiness, only the right to pursue it. Money may bring a surge of happiness, but it isn't lasting. Nor does it bring contentment. It's been said people who were asked how much money they would need to be comfortable responded twenty percent more than they currently had. This was at all levels of income.

So what does enrich us, make our lives full? It is up to us to capitalize on our equality. As Mark Twain said, "The secret of getting ahead is getting started." Maybe the answer is finding ways to use opportunities to increase our appreciation of the finer things and enjoy life to the maximum of our abilities. No matter what our occupation or situation is Tourism Writing can be a useful tool in this endeavor.

Tourism Writing allows the message of intriguing things about places and events to be told. It creates an awareness of another world ready to be explored by adventurous individuals. Then it offers a direct invitation to visit that world, along with a guide including photos and links. It does not matter whether the place is Repton, Alabama, or Bellingham, Washington, readers are exposed to events or places that may tweak their interest. While this book focuses on Alabama and nearby areas as examples, by extension all states have unique features. And even the smallest areas usually have local historians who can point out those interesting places or events to potential visitors, hopefully enticing them enough to visit.

Travel guides and advertisements appeal to many people but they are seen as one television ad or one ad on a sheet of paper. Not only is the image fleeting, there's also a barrier in place. The viewer knows the purpose is to make a sale, and it is often quickly dismissed for that reason. However, when a reader of a novel has established a rapport with a character and makes an emotional connection with what that character is experiencing at a real place or event, a new level of involvement occurs. The photos and links seem inadequate. Oftentimes, it stirs feelings deep enough to make a reader sufficiently curious to want to see the place or attend the event in person. Even more personal is the direct invitation to visit. Readers feel welcome. Then Tourism Writing has achieved its goal.

2
SCHOOLS

The most obvious way Tourism Writing can benefit people is in schools. Since this is a new genre, it can tweak students' curiosity. New types of assignments are refreshing and they stimulate interest. Since the project requires seeking a place or an event conducive to encouraging visitors to their area, students will find themselves either adding to their knowledge of a known location or special occasion, or searching and exploring something they know little about to see if it is worthy of consideration. They will have to research and analyze their options.

Reaction to investigation is automatic, if not reflex. Immediately upon investigating a location, you are likely to discover something previously unknown. For example, a student attending a Mardi Gras Parade in Mobile, Alabama, for the first time might be surprised to see a crowd of all ages scrambling for trinkets. Or, in researching its history, the student may uncover the fact that Mobile celebrated Mardi Gras first, before New Orleans.

My story, entitled *Raisin' Cain*, won the 2014 Southeastern Literary Tourism Initiative Contest (SELTI). It stimulated a lot of interest in showing how Mobile's Mardi Gras is family friendly. Hopefully, it also brought some new visitors who read it to Mobile. It is printed here as a sample.

RAISIN' CAIN

Mamie was ninety-three when she stepped onto the Cain Raisers' float on Joe Cain Day, the Sunday before Mardi Gras a couple of years ago. But that didn't stop her from throwing beads and Moon Pies and enjoying every minute of the ride through downtown Mobile, Alabama.

A transplant from Yankee Land, Mamie saw things about Mardi Gras that native Mobilians often miss. "When do you ever see a crowd of over a hundred thousand people this happy?" she asked me during the hour we parked beside the Mobile Municipal Auditorium, waiting in line with thirty other floats for the Joe Cain Parade that began in 1966 to start.

I mulled over that as our float finally moved forward. Chief Slacabamorinico, IV, pastor Bennett Wayne Dean, who'd held the position over twenty years, led the parade decked out in his colorful feathered headpiece. We eased through downtown streets of Mobile, all blocked off for the duration of the parade. The crowd's glee was evident as our float passed Bienville Square, packed twenty rows deep with smiling faces looking up at us.

Children and adults with outstretched arms screamed, "Throw me something, lady." Some had signs with a rider's name, or their own name, held high. Others had jar retrievers to scoop up throws, or upside-down umbrellas they hoped to fill.

At 96, still not too old for Mardi Gras.

One elderly lady in the front row sat in her wheelchair in a wide-brimmed hat. She could barely hold up her hands to wave at riders. But she didn't have to beg for anything. Maskers generously showered that person, probably a long-time parade-attendee, with full packages of beads, doubloons and anything else they could aim her way. Her lap was full.

Mamie was right. Where else are people so pleased to catch those trinkets? The float slowed to a stop and Mamie nudged me. "They even say, 'Thank you', and they share. Look over there." She pointed to a unkempt man in tattered clothes with a scruffy beard handing over his loot to the nearest child. I saw another person four rows back with a sign saying, "We're from Missouri. Show us what you've got." Next to him, a teenager held a big net. I barraged them with Moon Pies and beads, but missed my mark. Not one item fell into his net.

As we turned the corner on a narrow side street, our float was within inches of the crowd. It stopped again and a lady holding a child's hand spoke directly to me. Wide-eyed, she leaned across the barriers put there for safety and asked, "What's going on?"

A tipsy sailor next to her slurred, "Say, do you do this every weekend?"

As the float pulled away, I shook my head but I wondered if he believed me. I didn't have time to respond to the lady's question. I wasn't sure how to answer it anyhow. Couldn't she tell this was a parade?

We rounded another corner to a packed Government Street. As a main artery, traffic from Bankhead Tunnel usually flows down this street. Not today, and not before or after any Mardi Gras parades. Some days, we have as many as five parades. During this two-week season, vehicles are diverted to our other tunnel, the Wallace Tunnel on Interstate 10.

A policeman on horseback made his way to the beginning of the parade, evidently to bring it to another halt because we stopped again in front of the Admiral Semmes Hotel. Guests on the balcony screamed out their presence. Though it was a good distance away, some caught throws from maskers with strong arms. Gleefully, others snatched beads from outstretched hands of their companions and put them around their necks.

On the street below, men and women gave trinkets to people they'd probably befriended as they patiently awaited the grand spectacular. Many handed over things to people they never saw before and they'll never see again. Some stepped out of the way to watch the joy of a child catching a stuffed animal and hugging it close. Mamie looked at me and remarked, "It's not the trinkets they want, it's the thrill of the chase."

It's all free, too. The only expense may be for parking if no spots on the street are available. Homeowners or business establishments nearby fill their yards or parking lots with cars. At five or ten dollars a space, depending on how close they are to the parade route, they can pick up quite a few dollars during the two weeks of festivities.

While people await the colorful pageantry, they chat with each other. There are no strangers. The crowd of all ages is composed of every ethnic group, race and religion, from the very rich, such as a former Mardi Gras queen, to the very poor, even the homeless. During this equalizer, camaraderie abounds. In addition, all are entertained by vendors rolling squeaky carts down the street, hawking their wares. "Balloons, stuffed animals, hot popcorn."

Some entrepreneurs pull wagons with ice chests full of drinks. Others set up shop in tents and tempt potential customers with the scent of onions frying, and hamburgers, hot dogs, and sausages filling the air. Children beg for cotton candy when they get a whiff of its sugary aroma. Vendors flock to Mobile to make money. And they do.

Mardi Gras is also a big tailgate party. Near the auditorium, under the interstate, people with RV's and trailers rent spaces for the season. Other families gather on street corners, in parking lots, or at friends' houses. Setting up their own grills, they barbeque chicken, cook corn-on-the-cob, bake potatoes and munch on King Cake, feasting on the sumptuous food often washed down by beer, wine or mixed drinks that flow freely.

Children, who'll enjoy school holidays on Monday and Fat Tuesday, sip on soft drinks from decorated plastic cups caught the previous year, frolic around on the sidewalks, and climb ancient, huge oak trees until the parade arrives. Then, they're ready to do what they do best--yell out, "Moon Pie; beads!" and scramble.

On streets off the parade route, carnival rides like Ferris wheels go round and round. People stand in line awaiting their turn to ride and scream, sometimes in mock fear. Like other things behind the scene--such as the float building, the costumes, the formal rentals, sales of ball dresses, photography of events—all promote Mobile's economy.

Mardi Gras has other, long lasting benefits, too—sentimentality. Many memories are made by people who are lucky enough to live in Mobile or to come here to attend the festivities on a regular basis. When Mardi Gras is in session, ghosts of the past surface in the minds of people remembering times long gone. They hear echoes of those who marched these streets in bands to the cheers of the crowd, or of maskers riding in parades year after year as members of Mardi Gras Societies, responding to the crowd's pleas.

It has happened ever since 1867 when Joe Cain rode down Government Street in a decorated charcoal wagon pulled by a mule. Despite Union soldiers' efforts to stop him and his six fellow Confederate veterans, they made noise dragging rakes against iron work as they trekked down the main street of the city.

As is customary, in honor of Cain's revival of Mardi Gras after the Civil War, the parade came to a halt in front of the Church Street Graveyard. It stopped long enough for the black-clad and black-veiled Merry Widows to place a wreath on Joe Cain's grave where he was reburied in the 1960's.

Planning for this event is extensive. Artistic paper-mache floats conforming to the theme are a year long in the making. Costumes of riders also match. Discipline is needed. While police cars and motorcycles with sirens blasting clear the road, bands—including the hundred year-old Excelsior Band, some descendants of the predecessors—march between floats to slow down the parade. They always get a huge round of applause. Strutting drum majors' moves become contagious. Bystanders dance or tap their feet to the beat of the marching tunes, especially *When the Saints Go Marching in*.

One other place the parade almost comes to a standstill is a section set aside for those mentally or physically challenged. When we approached, Mamie said, "I can't wait for this. Catching throws makes them so happy; they're so easily pleased." Along with other maskers, she bombarded them with throws. "Look at that," she said, "even the most solemn crack a smile when they're handed an unwrapped moon pie or when beads are draped around their necks."

Mamie was right. For all involved, fun, fellowship and good times prevail. Few can resist. People get caught up in the frivolous event and forget their problems. Time stands still for Mardi Gras.

However, it comes to an end. After travelling an hour and a half long route on the streets of downtown Mobile, we pulled to a stop near the bus that transports us to our Mardi Gras Ball. Mamie looked at me. I saw a sparkle in her faded blue eyes when she was being helped off the float. "You know," she said, "This may be my last time to ride. But I've enjoyed every minute of these ten years." She raised her brows. "Before I moved to Mobile, I thought Mardi Gras was a drunken brawl. I know better now. I don't even drink, but I do have fun. The best part of it is giving others pleasure. It's amazing that one moment, one throw, such a small, insignificant thing like a string of beads, a Moon Pie, a cup, or a bag of peanuts can bring so much pleasure. It does. You can see pure joy in their eyes. Do you know what I mean?"

I nodded because I understood.

She took me by the arm. "My husband was military and we moved around a lot. Every place we were stationed, I studied the history and the culture. I soon learned that Mobile has a ton of history and a culture all its own. It ranks with the best of all the places I've lived. Somehow, I feel like I fit in here."

"My mother always said, 'If you get Mobile dirt on your feet you can never shake it off.'"

"Well, I guess she was right. Once I got here, I planned to return to retire, and I did." Mamie folded her arms and paused to face me. "Since I made Mobile my home, I researched even more of its history. I found out some things, too. In the past, like a lot of other people around the country, I thought New Orleans had the first Mardi Gras. But, I soon discovered Mobile has the oldest annual carnival celebration in the U.S. It started in 1703, fifteen years before New Orleans."

I didn't tell her I knew that. She smoothed back white hair set askew in the wind. As she slipped her arm back into the crook of my elbow, I slowed down to match my speed to her shuffle. Her heavily sequined costume in Mardi colors of purple and gold rustled as the pants legs rubbed together. Since we were behind the crowd, except for the busses rumbling away from the scene, it made the only sound on the now nearly silent street.

We reached our bus, and a teary-eyed, preschooler without any beads hanging on his neck caught Mamie's attention. As the boy's mother watched, she took all of the beads from around her own neck. "Here." She slipped them over his head. "Happy Mardi Gras."

"I couldn't find a place to park, so we missed his *first* parade," the mother explained. "Thank you so much. You made his day."

I glanced back at the emblem on the side of the float, a sketch of a tombstone reading, *R.I.P. Joe Cain.*

"Mamie," I said. You'll be here next year. Only Joe Cain's entitled to rest in peace.

She was.

In today's fast-paced world of multi-tasking and texting, it's difficult to retain students' attention. Teachers have to be entertainers, maybe even comedians. At a college level, especially when classes last four hours, the session needs variety. Even if a teacher could lecture the entire period, students stop listening after about twenty minutes, or less. Participation can't last too long; neither can visuals or exercises. In English classes, another option is writing, but the assignment needs to be interesting. Time-tested subjects work up to a point. Then a teacher needs to be innovative. Tourism Writing can fill this gap.

How? Tourism Writing provides a challenge. First, students have to delve deep to find the subject they want to discuss. Second, it must be one that will appeal to potential visitors, people outside their own comfort zone. Third, they should go to the place or event or read about it to gain detailed and unknown information. Fourth, they need to write about it using their research, perhaps pretending to be an individual who will benefit from attracting tourists. Fifth, they should write a polished, professional essay, appealing to individuals to stimulate interest in the area described.

To take the assignment a step farther, perhaps it could include finding a market for the essay, a way to send it to people who might become interested in visiting a place they've read about. Another possibility would be using social media for exposure. In any event, good will about a place or event could be spread.

Teachers benefit too. When reading and critiquing these essays, they learn more about the areas in which they live than they knew before. Some may simply be insignificant facts; however, others can provide real revelations. For example, an essay may clarify distances between cities, figures of exact populations, or the fact that locals play the parts in *To Kill a Mockingbird* in Monroeville, Alabama. For example, people in the audience seemed amused to discover that the local district attorney acted as the scoundrel in that play a few years ago.

Discussions of these topics are stimulating for teachers. Students often surprise them with perceptive observations regarding the subject matter. In sharing what they have learned, it's rewarding to see students inspire each other. It is also elating when students tell how visiting a place or event inspired them to pursue other cultural activities, or to explore venues they'd never before considered. Their enthusiasm for new adventures is contagious and rewarding.

One writing assignment that works at Faulkner University is our annual Tourism Poetry Contest. When it is first announced, a few students may moan and groan and say, "I don't like poetry," or "I can't write poetry," or "I can't make anything rhyme." Often, after a teacher compares poetry to songs, which most students can equate to, and explains that poetry doesn't have to rhyme, but it needs rhythm, a beat—along with emotion, imagery and symbols—the tune of the protestors often changes. Others welcome the chance to write a poem. One student quickly replied, "Oh, I'm excited. I love poetry; I know what I want to write about—the cruise terminal in Mobile." Then, there's the prizes, things like dinner and a movie donated by local businesses. That tweaks their interest, especially if you have prizes for first, second and third place winners.

Colleges with branches can allow students attending them to participate. This contest is not limited to English classes. It's open to almost any other discipline, such as history, speech, or psychology. All that entries need is a connection to unify the poem to the topic. Many of those connections are listed in this book by showing how different organizations or people of different occupations can benefit from tourism writing. Also, if the rules of the contest are kept simple, more people are likely to participate. A sample of the poetry contest guidelines is listed below:

FAULKNER UNIVERSITY
Tourism Poetry Contest
ALL Faulkner Students Encouraged to Enter
Submission Guidelines
People who claim they do not like, or understand, poetry will generally admit they like songs. Consider this: songs are words put into music; poetry is music put into words. All poetry contains emotion (feelings) and it often includes symbolism (one thing representing another) and imagery (a verbal picture of something). It does not have to rhyme but it needs rhythm – a beat like a song has.

The theme is the new genre of writing – **Tourism Literature**. Pick a particular place or event in your area and focus on why it is interesting in a way that appeals to a wide variety of readers. It may be serious or humorous, but entries must have appropriate content.

It must be original and not previously published

- It needs a title
- Length: Twelve to twenty-four lines / single spaced
- Cover Page with your name, address, phone number, e-mail address and title of poem. (Title should also appear at top of poem)
- Optional: include 2–3 pictures of place or event

A Sample Poem:

Close to Eden
I step on the rocks
And the water slaps my feet.
Makes me wonder how many
Other times the waves
Of Mobile Bay
Splashed against the feet of
People I'll never know.

Who were they,
And why were they here?
Like me, were they looking for
A moment of peace
Away from the cares
Of their lives?
If they were searching
For a spot
As close to Eden as possible,
Perhaps they found it.

Opening Date:

Closing Date:

 The 1st Place Winners from the participating locations will be announced on

 An event will be held for winners to read their poems.

 Grand Prize Winner will be chosen from the 4 first place winners.

 Schools definitely benefit from such endeavors. Developing a new way of writing is somewhat like an inventor unveiling a new device. If it works, it often makes the news, giving the schools involved good press. In the case of institutions of higher learning, presenting a course not offered before is intriguing. It appeals to prospective employers, high-quality teachers, parents of students, and the students themselves. Businessmen see value in imaginative thinking, teachers like challenges, parents understand the importance of staying up-to-date, and bored students, especially serious ones, look forward to trying new ideas. Routine becomes dull. People like to be on the cutting edge. It's stimulating. Colleges that take advantage of new programs such as this are considered progressive and people seek to attend them.

 This is especially true in the twenty-first century when older students frequently outnumber traditional ones. Many of these non-traditional students trying to improve their economic status have jobs and families. They don't have time for the mundane. In night classes, some who have worked an eight-hour day, or have come to school straight from a night shift, have trouble staying awake. They need stimulation to survive; they also need interesting material to work with. Tourism Writing can provide both.

3
STUDENTS

Students can be very perceptive; they will often surprise teachers. For example, an English Literature student gave this reply to writing a poem to enter in Faulkner University's Poetry Contest in 2017:

"One thing I'll remember about this class is how we were able to get into tourism writing. This is something I really enjoyed because I was able to incorporate something I like doing with something for school. I've always liked poetry and being able to be a part of it on a grander scale was great for me. I really hope in the near future I'll be able to participate in it again."

Such a statement is heartwarming. It was followed by other encouraging remarks. In an English 1302 class Courtney Blake had this to say:

"Sharing highlights on my city about its great landmarks is beneficial to me. Being able to provide tourists with great ideas about restaurants, shopping malls, background history, and family exhibits would be helpful in my career. I am honored to say it helps me in my field of duty...caring for the elderly who can't perform on their own."

She pointed out that Tourism Writing would be a way to share interesting information with her patients.

Another student, Savannah Easton, had different reasons for supporting Tourism Writing. She wrote:

"I'm originally from Corpus Christi, Texas, so a class on Tourism Writing about Mobile, Alabama, would be beneficial for me to learn about the culture here. I would love to learn about the history and different backgrounds of the people who grew up here. I work as a sales representative for AT&T U-verse and we talk to people from different areas of the United States. It would be nice to learn about different people from all over. Tourism Writing comes in handy learning about local attractions in Mobile—for example, the USS Alabama, Mobile downtown's history, and the Battle of Mobile Bay. Mardi Gras originated in Mobile and I would love to learn more about its history—how that came about. Overall, Tourism Writing would be valuable at Faulkner University."

Another opinion was given by Twanika Fountain:

"Tourism Writing has a lot of benefits. It can be in the form of landmarks we have in Alabama, such as the Exploreum, the cruise lines, Mobile Mardi Gras, music, and a host of other events in our great state. I work in the music business and there are a lot of cultures of music, such as rock and roll, blues and gospel. The Mobile Bay Fest was one great musical venture. Now, we have Bay Fest, the Rock and Roll Fest where local artists showcase their talents. Tourism Writing can make people aware of these attractions." Ten Sixty Five replaced Bay Fest.

Verlencia Lang, also a 1302 English student had this to say:

"I believe that Tourism Writing is important to me as a student because it is awesome to learn and understand our background and culture. As a Mobile native, the background and astonishing truth of Mardi Gras becomes important. Mobile, Alabama has tons of culture and hidden secrets lurking around every corner of this small, but big-hearted city. Tourism Writing can help inform potential visitors about what Mobile has to offer."

These heartfelt testimonials prove students can be stimulated with the right material.

4
TEACHERS

In Cullman, Alabama, fifty miles north of Birmingham, population 14,775, a science teacher and football coach at Cullman High School is capitalizing on an innovative idea of his own. Kyle Morris has planned a class called the Science of History. He is also very interested in Tourism Writing. As a native of Cullman proud of his city, he had clear opinions. "I think anything that can broaden my students knowledge of areas around the state is a great tool," he said. "In my class I will address many places that students may eventually want to visit on their own. A tourism guide for that area will give them an "insiders" view of the area. So maybe instead of going to a chain restaurant they end up at an Archibald's BBQ, or a Saw's Soul Kitchen, or Top Hat BBQ."

He didn't feel it would benefit him as a coach. "As far as that goes," he said, "there is not a lot of connection. I can get my players interested in the course because of my enthusiasm, but there isn't much crossover."

But he did feel it could benefit his school and help promote his new course.

"Tourism is a growing industry in Cullman. Years ago, Ave Maria Grotto was the only thing people came to see in my town. Now, we have several softball fields, hosting tournaments almost every weekend. There are concerts, and the Shrine of the Most Blessed Sacrament, the Cullman Stockyard who hosts several large cattle sales with many out of town guests. With all these people coming through Cullman, my hopes are that some fall in love with our town and move here and become contributing members of our society, and build their families here."

He also had strong feelings about how Tourism Writing could benefit his community and commented, "There are so many ways! Cullman is an area with so much going on, that you can literally find almost anything that interests you within our community. Do you like Country Music? How about the Mary Carter Paint Store mentioned in former Cullman Resident Hank Williams Jr's 1979 song *I've Got Rights*? Do you like spelunking? Bangor Cave is located just 15 miles from Cullman, and once served as a nightclub and speakeasy! Do you enjoy hiking? Hurricane Creek Hiking Trails are minutes from downtown Cullman? Microbreweries? Goat Island Brewing is a locally owned and started brewery with a large taproom. Are you interested in Catholic Traditions? The Shrine of the Most Blessed Sacrament is located in Hanceville, less than 10 miles from Cullman, and Ave Maria Grotto, as well as St. Bernard Abby is located within Cullman. Johnny's BBQ has been voted one of Alabama's best BBQ's several times It's run by local Cullman folks. Do you like watersports? Lewis-Smith Lake is located in Cullman County and features some world-class bass and striper fishing, as well as crystal clear water, perfect for fun on a boat. What about a bakery that once functioned as a front for illegal alcohol sales? Currently it makes the world's best donut at Duchess Bakery in downtown Cullman. I could go on forever about the great things in my town!" The variety of attractions he listed shows he had no reluctance to promote his hometown.

He even had ideas about the best way to market the concept to have Tourism Writing courses added to school curriculum. He understood that his new class and Tourism Writing are both innovative and that if one works, the other would.

"I think that you have a definite possibility," he said. "So much of today's standardized testing, that makes or breaks students college applications, is based on writing. Having students write in something they know can help build these skills, while expanding the town's library of great info about itself."

visitcullman.org

Kyle Morris's opinions are likely to be reflected in those of many others, people who are proud of their towns and want to share their city's interesting attributes. Tourism Writing can help offer them that option.

Teachers have a certain curriculum they have to follow, but they also have their own styles and ways of approaching a subject. Also, in specialized fields, some leeway exists. One high school teacher who placed students in jobs commented on how Tourism Writing could be helpful in this endeavor.

Margaret Daniels, retired teacher/coordinator in Marketing and Sales commented, "I do not recall anything about Tourism Writing being taught in the schools when I was actively teaching. Mobile is ideally located and has many attractions to interest tourists with the possibility of even more to come. This possibility could increase the job market for co-op students as well as graduates. The more people know about their city's history, the better they can represent it to potential tourists, encouraging them to visit."

Paraphrasing an old adage, if you don't toot your own horn, who will? In fact, nobody else *can* do that for you. Pride in your hometown, or the place you've chosen to live, is not a sin. Besides, we can't take credit for its existence. In most cases, generations of people had a part in developing an area or establishing a city. Centuries ago, our forefathers cut through woods, fighting foes and animals, along with the unknown, to carve out a spot to inhabit. Never knowing what was around the curve, behind the next bush, or down the stream, they ventured across the plains, over the hills, valleys and mountains, and endless waterways, working their way west. On the route, they endured the unbearable and suffered hunger, sickness and death to develop this new land. In honor of their memory, their brave exploration of these United States of America, don't we have a right to invite others to also explore it and enjoy its unique spots of interest?

We have the perfect tool to do so—Tourism Writing. Not by following in their dangerous footsteps on a path that may be doomed, but by sitting in the comfort of a padded chair, typing words on a computer word processor, telling the history of those who went before, the men and women who forged the path, carved the statues, moved the battleships back to bays they defended, preserved old forts, planted the gardens, or gathered for the first Mardi Gras Parade.

We can't live our lives backwards. Nor can we retrieve what is lost. Once an historical site has been demolished, it is gone. We can build a replica, but it's not the same. If it's a fort, we may be standing on the same spot of ground where a soldier stood aiming his rifle, but we can't peek through the turret that's been torn down.

History is preserved by the efforts of those who value the past. What makes this happen? Edmund Burke said, "Those who don't know history are destined to repeat it." So, only those who know history and appreciate it enough to understand its importance are our hope. Facts in writing tend to impress people and to lead them to take action.

The next step is to make those facts available to interested people. So, the more Tourism Writing is promoted, the better off we'll all be, at least those of us who want to preserve our past and protect our future.

One way students can benefit from Tourism Writing is learning how to write in this genre. Once they learn how, they will probably do so, opening a new world to readers. If it becomes popular, the spin-off will be that established authors will most likely follow suit and add a new dimension to their work.

Vinson J. Bradley, director of enrollment for evening studies at Huntingdon College, saw additional benefits for students. He said, "Tourism Writing will make students more aware of what we have in this area. It will make them venture off campus and learn things nobody told them about. They'll learn to appreciate where they live more."

He was referring to Baldwin County, Alabama and he gave an example: "A couple of years ago, a student who lived on campus thought Bay Minette was from the campus to Wal Mart. He didn't know if you turn right at McDonald's, you'll find the court house." A history major in college, Bradley elaborated on that particular point of interest. "A lot of people don't realize what they see is built on top of a new court house. It has the original floors and features of the original courthouse. This is just one example. Every town has something unique that's not being talked about. And if it isn't, it will get lost. It's a shame some authors are reluctant to use real places and people in their stories. It's important to preserve treasures so they won't be forgotten." Tourism Writing could be the rescuer.

When asked how he feels students would respond to Tourism Writing, he replied, "It depends on how teachers present it. Most students are intrigued with something new. They instinctively have curiosity and will ask questions." Almost anything new is better than routine. This has proven true with the poetry contest at Faulkner University. The novelty of a different type of writing excites and motivates the students. They approach the task with gusto.

The University of South Alabama was founded in May, 1963 with Dr. Frederick Palmer Whiddon as its president. Although citizens protested the location in an area known as Wheelerville, saying it did not have a good reputation and was too far away from the population, the university owned the land, so they used it. Citizens were proven wrong; USA is now Mobile's second largest employer with over 5,500 employees and 16,699 students. The school has awarded over 80,000 degrees since its inception. University owned hospitals also treat over 250,000 patients annually. Serving until 1998, Dr. Whiddon, a progressive thinker, led the college to its present success. He also invested in the success of the community by serving in many other organizations.

His daughter, Karen Whiddon Peterson, followed in his footsteps and those of her mother, who taught elementary school. As a member of an academic family, she is a senior instructor at USA working on her Ph.D at South. She and her mother also wrote a young adult book.

She feels Tourism Writing could be beneficial to students in more ways than one.

"Many students who come from all over the state and those from Mobile don't know about the city they will live in. I think it's intriguing to know about the area and write about it. It helps them make a connection. This keeps students in the state if they're more connected." She felt it is important for graduates to remain in Alabama because "Taxpayers have invested in their education. Anything connected to the area benefits all. This also applies to international students."

She added, "It benefits the whole state's economy if people stay here. It also helps them become aware of their surroundings, people they react with daily. I believe in cultural literacy. If you learn about people it leads to understanding." She felt this applied to the current controversy about Confederate statues and mentioned that there were "few Confederate slave holders." She spoke of inequities. Referring to General Robert E. Lee, she said, "Lee had his property stolen to be used as Arlington National Cemetery. Another thing, I'm a big proponent of freedom of speech. Mark Twain fought slavery and it's too bad he was censored because of the use of one word."

It is interesting that Peterson had her students use a form of Tourism Writing. "We had a scavenger hunt. Students went to places they passed daily, researched, and wrote about them. Some were historical buildings or plantations. We have lots of Greek supporters in Mobile. One was the statue of the Greek physician Tholos. It's made from the same marble originally mined from Greece. This very important symbol for Arts and Science stands on campus southeast of the Whiddon Administration Building." Such hands-on experience is very close to Tourism Writing.

Another possibility for a topic is a massive twelve-foot globe that once was the centerpiece in the Waterman Building's lobby. One day, after Commercial Guaranty Banking Company purchased the building in 1970, Dr. Whiddon received a phone call from a worker saying they had cut the globe in half and it was on the loading dock about to be trashed. Dr. Whiddon immediately sent for it and rescued it. "It took years to put together but now it still turns and it is surrounded by rails, just as it was in the Waterman Building," Peterson said. "When it was restored, the Airport Authority wanted it." But they didn't get it. It is now on display in the Mitchell Center at USA. Had it not been for a worker interested in saving history, this icon would have been lost.

The European-style Saenger Theater, which opened in 1927 and closed in 1970, was also about to be torn down when, with foresight, USA purchased it on the eve of its demolition and restored it. In 1999, after Whiddon had retired, it was sold back to the City of Mobile for one million dollars. The preserved historical building referred to as "Alabama's greatest showplace," is used on a regular basis. It would be a good topic for Tourism Writing, too.

Writing about such places also helps preserve them and allows visitors to take a walk into the past. Progressive teachers like Karen Peterson, who are willing to use innovative concepts, can help make this happen.

5
BUSINESS

As a native Mobilian, I am proud of my city. It comes natural to me to brag about it. It also pleases me when visitors comment on its beauty. This happened recently in downtown Mobile. A visitor passing by pointed to Cathedral Square and said, "You have a beautiful city here." I agreed. We chatted and he mentioned that he was in town on business.

"I read a lot of history books, but haven't come across much about Mobile," he said. "What year was it founded?"

After replying, 1702, I took the opportunity to tell him about some historical sites nearby. He seemed interested in them; I hope he had a chance to visit a couple.

This encounter reinforced my belief that more novels could refer to real places and events, not just metropolitan areas like New Orleans and Chicago, or major events like the St. Patrick's Day Parade in New York City or the Super Bowl wherever it takes place, but also to smaller, local happenings, those closer to home that visitors, or people living nearby, might enjoy by taking a short drive. For southerners, a few that come to mind are the fireflies in Elkmont, Tennessee in June, the Dismals Canyon glowworms in Franklin County, Alabama and the cheniers in southwest Lousiana. Although these events or unique places seem to be known by many and draw crowds, some people who would be interested have never heard of them.

Many of these places are part of nature and free and open to the public. Some you can simply drive through. President Theodore Roosevelt had much foresight when he started the National Parks System and preserved the beauty of nature for future generations. The cost for a pass to visit them is minimal and they exist all over our country. Also, most historical places in Washington, D.C., are free and open to the public. There's much of interest there for visitors. But this is true of practically any area of the United States. One such place is the oldest Church of Christ in Alabama. It was built in 1811 in Rocky Springs in Jackson County. The wooden building still stands.

Almost any place you go, you can find something unique. But such information isn't always available at a Welcome Center. Sometimes those secrets are well hidden and you have to ask around and find a local person who is interested in their own history or legacy. They'll usually welcome the opportunity to tell you about it in a folksy way a formally written travel guide could never accomplish. Or you might learn about such places in advance of a visit, if they are woven into Tourism Writing.

In the past, as a weekly newspaper columnist, I had plenty of opportunities to tout my hometown. To report on a noteworthy event oftentimes involved something interesting as part of the story. If not, sometimes I'd find a way to sneak it in. Once, when I was covering the Blessing of the Fleet at Bayou La Batre, AL, a woman boarding a fishing boat slipped into the water. She was saved, but soaking wet. They retrieved her purse, but she kept looking back at the water, asking, "Where's my scarf? I just bought it yesterday." Sometimes little things like that add humor to a serious situation. Then the place is often remembered and maybe it creates an interest in visiting the area to see where something happened. Peculiar things often trigger curiosity. My interest in visiting Honduras is explained in the following story.

Sometimes things occur for odd reasons. There's a place I want to write about that was not my destination, but I went there once—for about ten minutes. My husband and I were on a trip to Costa Rica and the plane made several stops along the way, as many times as we were served a meal of beans. The announcements were in Spanish. If they repeated them in English, it wasn't recognizable to me. On the fourth landing, I looked out the window and discovered the buildings in the airport had no identification, but this airport was larger than the rest. "This must be Costa Rica," I told my husband. We retrieved our luggage and deplaned.

In the long line for customs, I heard the two young girls in front of us speaking English and I chatted with them for a minute before asking, "Is Costa Rica your home?"

Wrinkling her brow, one of them shook her head. "No, I live right here in Honduras."

My eyes widened. I snatched up my luggage and headed for our plane that was still on the tarmac, followed closely by my husband. Much to our relief, we made it back on board before it took off.

My curiosity was sparked. I decided right then to return someday, see what I missed, find a unique place, and write a story about it. Maybe I'll feature fields where they grow those beans. But I haven't returned yet. When I do, perhaps I can tell my story and convince city leaders that their airport needs "Honduras" visible on a building that can be seen from the landing field.

I also developed an interest in sites of famous trials after witnessing a bank robbery once. This extended to the imaginary trial in *To Kill a Mockingbird*, so I went to the play in Monroeville, Alabama a couple of years ago. It was a different type of crime from the one I'd witnessed, but it brought back memories of that unpleasant experience. And I was finally able to write about it.

When do bank robberies get personal? When you, or a family member, is in the bank staring at a gun barrel.

Years ago, my son happened to be in a bank when it was robbed. He'd walked down the street from our business to the bank only a block away. With my other children in the car, I drove there to pick him up. On the way, I passed two men with bags in their hands hustling along. One of them, I recognized but it wasn't a pleasant memory, so I made no effort to speak to him. I simply looked away.

Leaving my children in the car, I went inside to see why Rick wasn't waiting for me outside. I quickly discovered why. The police arrived in mass, locked all the doors saying the bank had been robbed and started their questioning. Rick said one of the two men had vaulted over the counter and "the other one had the gun in my ribs."

I became shaky but knew I had to get back to my other children in the car and be calm about it. When I was allowed to leave and found my children safe, one told me, "We were on the radio. A reporter asked us about those robbers. I told them I saw them." Uh, oh!

As I drove home, I discovered the children had also been questioned by the police. The oldest one, Mike, had described the men he saw. Then I recalled another problem. The night before a neighbor's son who wasn't old enough to drive, took his mother's car and raced around our neighborhood going a hundred miles per hour. He hit a pine tree in my front yard and sailed into a large oak tree next door. I'd cleaned out my desk the day before and had puts small receipts in the garbage. It was on the street, got knocked over and papers were scattered the full one hundred feet along the edge of our lot. I knew the FBI was coming to show me photos. So as soon as we got home, we all hustled to gather the trash.

The young man driving the car had awakened me at 3 a.m. when he telephoned to tell me the police were in front of my house. I recognized his voice and was right in assuming he'd fled the scene. I was tired when the agents came to show me photos, but I found the two men's pictures, identified both, and told the police the story about one of them.

"He was dating a lady who worked for me," I said, "and he came to my house to the only office party we ever had." I told the agent that another guest who made the evening memorable by dropping her cigarette and burning a hole in my brand new sofa said that man and his date helped themselves to refreshments before I entered the room. I pointed to a corner in my family room . "He sat right there all evening."

The agent said this was a family of bank robbers raising their bail for the last robbery. The news didn't surprise me. The man was cruddy looking and I never trusted him. It was against my better judgment to let him in my house, but our employee persuaded me.

In the weeks before the criminals were apprehended, FBI agents went to my son Mike's school and took him to a motel to identify somebody. I think that helped their case. Later, during the weeklong trial, two unexpected things happened. First, the defense brought in our former employee claiming I remembered him from being at my house, not from the robbery. I quashed that theory. Next, when the two men were convicted, I hung around to see what their sentences would be—both got more than a dozen years in prison. I chatted with a man sitting next to me a few minutes and was ready to leave when I was called into the judges chambers. The men just sentenced were a couple of feet opposite me. The defense attorney said I was talking to the husband of a juror. By then, I was angry, I insisted that I didn't know who the man was and that we weren't talking about the trial. Then I blurted out, "I'm a dismissed witness, Judge, and my parking time is almost up. If you don't let me go, and I get a ticket, I'm bringing it to you." I was allowed to leave. I didn't get a parking ticket, so I never saw that judge again. Maybe if I had, I would have tried to find out if those men served their terms or if they're still living by their wits and terrorizing innocent victims. But, they may both be dead.

Interest in Tourism Writing is not limited to any age group. People of all generations can be involved. Youth have a natural curiosity and are often intrigued by the world and the way things work. We took a tour of Alabama a few years ago mapped out by my teen-aged daughter. She'd marked all of the historical places. One was Jay Plantation where William B. Travis, a cohort of Davey Crockett, once lived. However, when we reached it, the lady who lived there said it was closed to visitors. Nonetheless, she let us tour the property and even told us the story of two men who'd drowned in a vat of wine in the attic. One of my sons, a ham radio operator, only wanted to see towers and he could spot them a mile away. All in all, it was a great trip and a wonderful learning experience.

Another point of view showing the benefits of Tourism Writing comes from Ben Davis, a retired engineer. He says, "We are the Baby Boomers, the generation that rode *en masse* to change the world. Though we may have lost a little of the spunk of our youth, our curiosity has waned but little. Active community tourism provides a forum for the information we crave to learn of areas and places where we might broaden our knowledge of the rich histories, cultures, and charms we have yet to experience." Profound words. As long as we live, we should continue learning. New experiences keep us vibrant and make the difference between simply existing and truly living.

Mobile proudly welcomes a new service many may not know about. In the fall of 2017, Auburn University's School of Industrial and Graphic Design will offer hands-on experience to fifteen students when they open Futures Studio, an innovative concept. These students will work with local businesses and industry to develop, brand, package and market local products or services. While immersed in the culture of a problem, they will design a solution for it. This should attract young people with talent to work and live in Mobile. First, though, the word has to be spread. (http://www.cityof-mobile.org/news.php?view=full&news-2778)

Robert Kirby is a person who has every reason to know the importance of Tourism Writing. As the former President of the Better Business Bureau of South Alabama, his job was to keep citizens happy and to encourage new business to locate in the area.

"Tourism is important to any community, and tourists need to feel safe," he said. He gave an example of what made him feel the Mobile area is safe. "We had to move out of our home for two years after Hurricane Katrina. During that time, nothing bad happened to it." He stressed that feeling safe "encourages visitors to return, or even to relocate in an area. Communities do compete with each other. If people get the impression that a community cares about visitors, or read a book that makes them feel that way, they're more likely to visit or to choose to live there."

Kirby said when he came to Mobile from Indiana in 1970 he know nothing about the city. "People away from here know little about Mobile and the Gulf Coast. Some don't even know about our waterways and beaches and the climate." He did know he'd have a place to sail his boat. However, when he mentioned sailing in the Mobile area to a friend, the man asked, "There's water there?"

Then, he spoke of the present. "We are now getting industry here and any way we can inform people of its potential is good. Tourism writing can be a big help. It's a way to get the message out."

When asked how Tourism Writing could best be marketed to colleges, he said he felt colleges "need more factual information about areas," adding, "the public image of Alabama in the North and West is not good. Colleges and universities need to step up with knowledge about Mobile and the Gulf Coast. Communities in general need business and clean industry. With more of that, we'll have more tourists."

His viewpoint as a deacon in his church is that many people today feel there's more to life than "partying" and visitors may be looking for a place to worship when scouting a city to relocate in or when simply on vacation.

To sum up, he said, "We should send the message to visit Mobile and South Alabama and bring your money." That can be accomplished with Tourism Writing. Taking in money is important; even preachers, priests, and rabbis have to be paid. And all churches can't accept gambling chips in the collection as they do in Las Vegas.

One person in Economic Development helps send this message, director of the Mobile Film Office assists film producers in finding suitable locations in the area. Eva Golson and her location coordinator, Diane Hall, read the scripts and then scout the area for the most appropriate locations to film.

The first film Golson worked on was *Close Encounters of the Third Kind* in 1977 "That put Mobile on the map," she said, noting that it became a blockbuster hit. Although the hangers where it was filmed are now being used, visitors can at least see the buildings. Another location popular with producers is the Battleship Alabama where the movie *Under Siege* was filmed, which celebrated its commission 75 years ago on August 12, 2017. It is sought after for more than movies—such as TV documentaries, travel or commercials. Visitors can see it and board the ship. Then history is combined with fantasy.

Golson considered it exciting to meet Robert Mitchum and Nicholas Cage. She feels people often don't understand why actors can't stop and talk to them. "Sometimes they're in the middle of a scene," she says and added, "I never talk to them unless I'm sure they're not in a scene. She also said people often confuse actors with the characters they play. "They don't understand their personality," she added.

But she found a man who does and recommended him to be a security driver for actors who come to Mobile. Sonny McCoy, a retired corporal with the Mobile Police Department with twenty-seven years service, has driven stars like Robert De Niro, Jeffrey Morgan, Dave Bautista, and many others, feels that he and Nicolas Cage have established good rapport. "We have a sense of humor together." McCoy is professional when driving Cage, and feels that a younger aspiring actor might be star-struck and annoy a man like Cage. However, he did admit they talk about personal things at times. "But when my friends ask me what we talk about, I tell them, 'It's personal. It stays in the car.'

When interviewed for the job, McCoy said he told Cage, "It's an honor and a privilege to be your driver. I promise I won't bother you. It's my *job*."

Dolph Lundgren, a Russian boxer in a *Rocky* movie, made McCoy proud when he stayed in Mobile an extra day to be driven around and shown Mobile's attractions and history. And he found it amusing that Robert De Niro couldn't seem to remember his name was Sonny and kept asking after each question about places, "And your name again?". Finally, McCoy answered De Niro's third question adding, "And my name's Sonny."

His personality made him popular. McCoy spent years stationed on the parade route downtown during Mardi Gras and became known as the "Hula Hoop Cop" because he twirled the hoop each year in full uniform. "I'd have people ask to take pictures with me, but the best part was when kids would come out and start twirling that hoop. People would clap. I enjoyed it."

His favorite memory of Cage was the first time he drove him to a base camp trailer on Airport Boulevard to a restaurant parking lot behind Mobile Police Headquarters. Two ladies and a little girl were waiting to see them pass "to get a look at Cage," McCoy said. When Cage went inside, the little girl approached McCoy, asking if he'd take a photo with her. When he asked why, she said, "Because I want a picture with Nick Cage's driver."

"When Nick got back to the car, as we drove away, I told him about it and he said, 'Stop the car.' He got out and asked the girl's mom, 'Is it okay if I take a picture with your daughter?'" McCoy laughed. "Seems like the mother called WKRG and it was on the news." He paused. "But Nick is all about anything to do with kids. He says, 'They made me what I am today.'"

Since McCoy and his wife love to travel and he says, "We research places first," maybe Tourism Writing can help them find interesting places and decide where they'll go and what they'll do next. That is whenever he's not busy driving Nicholas Cage and other famous stars around.

The list of Movie and TV Production Filmed in Mobile is five pages long and highly diversified. *The Cowboy Way: Alabama*, TV Series INSP/Glassman Media premiers August 10, 2017. "The second season was in the works before season one aired," Golson said, proud that this is one of many films to be produced in the future.

On a lighter note, Golson recalled an amusing incident. "One person filming a TV series asked if we could shut down Interstate 10." She smiled. "And it was not even a network show." Some people's expectations go beyond the norm. But, as the expression states, "The show must go on." And if you let tourists know about something to see or do in your area, they'll visit, and return.

Director of Marketing for Faulkner University Ron Lambert expressed his viewpoint of the benefits of Tourism Writing. He stressed that it's important to differentiate yourself in marketing a product. He said, "The basic marketing principle in a course is that you have to stand out in a crowd." Tourism Writing can get readers *to* visit places they read about because it highlights what is different about an area or an event and people need examples to rely on to interest them.

He gave an example of how this is effective: "In the old movie, *E T*, you saw them eating Reece's Pieces, not M & M's. The same is true with James Bond's cars. Among them are the Alfa Romero, Aston Martin, Bentley and Rolls Royce. *Big Fish* used Bibb Graves Bridge in Wetumpka, AL. The product placement now is when companies or cities like Los Angeles give discounts to filmmakers. Companies pay to have their products placed in movies and cities also pay to have their names used. It could be a very big deal. Forest Gump used some real names but not in every case. Put an actual city in a story and the city pays, cities compete to make their own places important and more interesting to visitors than other places."

When asked how to market Tourism Writing, his approach was straightforward.

"Go where the money is. Show students' interest. Colleges build courses around that—students asking for courses. It's all about demand." Tourism Writing has the added benefit of being interdisciplinary; it works in history, theater, hospitality, tourism and other departments. It is not confined to English courses. The spin-off is that students of Tourism Writing who later become authors will write about places using it.

It needs to be taken a step farther. If famous authors start writing in this genre, it will quickly gain appeal. But that needs impetus to work. "To get established authors to write Tourism Writing and become involved you must first prove it works," Lambert said. This is viable because Tourism Writing is different in itself. It evokes emotion and people connect with places the photos show and those referred to by the links. It gives a complete picture. Since economic development and outcome is highly dependent on tourism, using an innovative way to increase interest in an area can be vital to its growth.

Nothing remains status quo. We either move forward or backward. It's a choice that requires action. So it befits us to take the best option and make the change and the effort to do what it takes to progress, not regress.

This is evidenced in Mayor Sandy Stimpson's proposed budget for the City of Mobile that he outlined at a press conference May 17, 2017. Three terms he included were a pay increase of five-thousand dollars a year across the board for policemen, allocating one million dollars for Mobile Fire-Rescue for use at the discretion of the interim chief, and twenty-three million to repair streets, parks, sidewalks, and bridges (WKRG.com).

These improvements will not only benefit citizens, they will also make Mobile more appealing to visitors. But it works both ways. To make such improvements depends on the city generating more revenue. What better way to do that than from tourists? The way tourists can find out about how Mobile's improvements make it a more appealing place to visit is through Tourism Writing.

For example, a novel set in Mobile could include a scene of someone being detoured because a street with uneven, cracked concrete—such as Glenwood—is being resurfaced. Another scene could show the Cochrane-Africatown Bridge being repaired. Working real places or events into a novel simply takes a little imagination.

And what better way to reach potential visitors to expose them to Mobile's attractions than Tourism Writing?

The spin-off is more jobs to fuel the economy. Success breeds success and this is true in the business world. We need the rich to start the businesses thereby providing jobs for the poor. Without the entrepreneurs in our country, we would be lost. Money can be made in almost any field. McDonald's is proof of that. Making a fortune selling hamburgers was highly improbable, yet it happened. But businesses are not started without someone taking a gamble. Oftentimes, individuals risk entire life savings. Sometimes it works; sometimes it doesn't. Maybe Tourism Writing could enhance a person's chance of success.

However, success or failure isn't restricted to businesses. It also applies to cities large and small. In the book *Marketing Places*, by Philip Kotler, Donald H. Haider and Irving Rein, it states, "Smaller cities and towns are also prone to decline. They often find themselves too dependent on one main source of revenue; when it dries up, so does the place. Young people move away after their high school graduation, and the place starts to resemble a retirement community" (p 7). It seems that smaller places suffer such difficulties with limited options to resolve them. Yet, some problems can be dealt with. If those towns were written about, it is likely that the free advertising would pay off. Revenue generated by tourists could fill the gap.

Although David Clark is not a native Mobilian—you have to be born here to qualify—he has been in Alabama since 1987. He served as Director of the Grand Hotel in Point Clear, AL for twenty-five years. Now, as President and CEO of Visit Mobile, he discussed the value of Tourism Writing, saying, "Anything anyone writes about the value of tourism educates all. It shows what the state has to offer by telling a story." He said his job is to get people to come experience Mobile's history, culture, cuisine and lodging using a balanced approach. "If I do my job right, people who come here to work, such as those who attend conventions, will want to return after seeing how they can also enjoy our city in a state of leisure." In other words, those who learn Mobile is a "neat" city with a variety of things to offer will want to return to "play" here.

Clark cited four components Mobile has that can make it sustain its ability to be successful as a destination: For accessibility, I 65, which begins in Mobile, water, an airport within fourteen miles, and Southern Hospitality. Bonus attractions include Mardi Gras, Bellingrath Gardens, the Battleship, and many seafood restaurants.

"Mobile has 3.2 million visitors a year and they spend 1.3 million dollars in Mobile. That provided 17 thousand jobs. In Alabama, tourists spend 13.5 billion dollars a year. It's a big industry, one we want to capitalize on. Mobile also has great health and good educational facilities, including USA, Mobile College, Spring Hill College, and Bishop State College. We have plenty of industry and are adding to that list every year. In addition, our city is relatively safe and that is constantly improving."

Clark told a story of Mobile being known better than is commonly thought. "I was in Washington D.C. in a cab and the driver asked where I was from," he said. "When I told him, his eyes lit up. 'I've been there. People talk to you. They speak to you on the street. When I came back to D.C. and tried to do the same, my friends thought I was crazy. I want to go back and meet a woman to be my wife in Mobile and live there.'"

He stressed that Mobilians do a good job of taking care of each other, citing an incident that happened when he worked at the Grand Hotel or the Riverview. He said the owner, David Bonner, wanted him to schedule a t-time so he could play golf but he told Clark to make sure he wasn't taking a t-time away from a customer or guest to work him in. "If residents take care of tourists, they'll take care of you," Clark said in praise of Bonner's unselfish attitude.

Clark suggested that Tourism Writing has the opportunity to paint a picture of Mobile as a tourism destination by creating an image of leisure. When thoughts of the city first come to mind, potential visitors can identify with it. "An iconic image wins over other people, if their quick reference includes Mobile's Port City reputation—Delta cruises and DUCK boats." He added that a ferry from Mobile to Fairhope and Gulf Shores running on a regular schedule would be a huge added attraction.

Clark lives in downtown Mobile, in the city's vibrant district, once almost abandoned but now thriving. He wants to be where he can best do his job by promoting it and he does that with a passion. Under his leadership, Mobile, Alabama, established in 1702, has a prodigious future.

BUSINESS 〉 **47**

Downtown Mobile.

Bienville Square.

Bankhead Tunnel.

6
TOURISM

The group who may profit equally with students and schools is the tourism business. John O'Melveny Woods, President of Intellect Publishing Company, said that Tourism Writing "can raise awareness of the quality of southern publishing. The South gets a bad reputation because of the way the media portrays it and the people who live there. Better press puts writers in a better light as to how writers are perceived."

If the tourism industry realizes this, then it will be in their best interest to help Tourism Writing with a marketing plan to get the support of the community. Things can move very fast for them. In turn, that would propel the entire concept forward. Things aren't always easy but they can be done. I am reminded of an amusing incident that happened to me and I had to find a way to solve the problem.

When my children were young, we always had a dog. Once in a while a cat, or gerbils, and birds were in the mix, but then, along came a rabbit. When I went to pick it up, I didn't have a cage, but I brought along a small cardboard box. I was only a mile from my home, so I wasn't concerned about a little rabbit hopping out on the floorboard of my car. What could happen in that short distance?

I soon discovered I should have been concerned. The person giving away the pet insisted that I had to take at least three. Within a block, the short trip turned longer. Traffic was heavy; every traffic light was red, and the little creatures climbed on top of each other and got out of that box. Darting all over from the back to the front seat, they tried to settle under the gas or brake pedals or in my lap. I'd squash one if I had to stop suddenly.

I slowed to a snail's pace and braked often. Once, with a rabbit crawling up my pants' leg, I jerked the steering wheel to pull to the curb. Drivers in cars behind me tooted horns and waved fists. They couldn't see the rabbits and they didn't know what was going on. They must have thought I was crazy or drunk.

But I found a solution. I pulled into somebody's driveway, gathered up the rabbits one by one and stuck them into my trunk. Luckily, none escaped, but I wouldn't have cared if they did, even though I'd hate to have seen the cute little balls of fur crushed by a car.

When I finally reached home without a casualty and herded those animals into a cage, I was hard pressed to resist a temptation. I'd never skinned a rabbit in my life. Only that, and the "Oos" and "Aws" of my children as they petted the furry critters, stopped me from having rabbit stew for dinner.

This occurrence convinced me that with determination goals can be accomplished. This applies to the goal of promoting Tourism Writing. It can also be achieved with perseverance and the support of interested parties—schools, students, people in the tourism business, politicians, and the entire community.

When asked about how Tourism Writing could benefit people in her profession, Myrna Green, who has spent forty-five years as Manager of Hancock County Tourism Development, said, "You'd be surprised at how many tourist don't know what tourism means. They don't know the difference between the Tourism Department and the Chamber of Commerce." She added, "You try to get the word out about how important tourism is by pointing out that tourists buy Cokes at the gas station and that gives the clerk there the money to buy something at Wal Mart. Fresh money turns over eight to thirteen times." She paused. "People ask me, 'What do you do?" They think it's little or nothing until I give them examples. One of the things is to get grants for Deep Water Horizon claims after the BP spill."

It is far-reaching. One was a claim from a shrimp boat captain who claimed he was out of work six months. Another was about the economic impact showing how the Tourism Bureau's hard claim of how many tourists *didn't* come to the area. Money was allocated to go to the tourism industry after they filed claims.

In the small, rural Hancock County, which uses volunteers and does not have a big budget, the BP grant was a blessing. "You get to people who don't know you. More find out about you and come to Mississippi. The grant enabled the Tourism Bureau to advertise on WWL. Without that money, they couldn't have afforded to advertise because the cost was prohibitive. It provides a connection otherwise unavailable. "This illustrates how important tourism is to people who don't understand," she said. Tourism Writing could serve the same purpose.

When speaking to schools, she tells students, "Be an ambassador for your community," pinpointing their interest by asking, "What's your favorite place?" She chuckled at recalling one reply from a teenaged female, "Some mountain in Georgia." If the girl meant Stone Mountain in Atlanta, it must not have impressed her enough to remember the name.

Ms. Green also lets her listeners know what qualifies a person as a tourist. "When your grandma visits and you take her out to eat, she becomes a tourist." This is followed by, "It's hard to make the general public understand the importance of tourism." She shook her head. "Many don't know."

More Tourism Writing will make people want to go places. In Hancock County, Ms. Green said they had to start Africatown over and create a tourism file. "You have to know what visitors want to see, what interests them, and they'll tell other visitors. One thing she was proud of was the Angel Trees carved from trees people hung onto during Katrina to survive. Tears welled up in her eyes. "People owe their lives to those trees. They're carved with chain saws. People come from far away to take photos of them."

Ms. Green's ideas of how to get courses in Tourism Writing included in the curriculum were, "Those courses should be taught to make students realize exactly what tourism is and what a huge economic impact it has. Sixteen point four percent of the people on the Mississippi Gulf Coast work force is in tourism. You have to teach people about classes in hospitality. Kids say, 'There ain't nothin' here,' because they aren't aware of what is in their area. Writers should be accurate about what *is* here." She added an important plus, "And the service industry is still hiring in a time when jobs are hard to find."

She gave a personal example of how a menial job shouldn't be turned down because it can lead to a lucrative career. "My son was out of college and needed a job. I told him to go to a hotel and take *any* job he was offered. They have tremendous turn over. He was hired for two nights a week as night auditor. Next, he drove the airport shuttle where he met someone new in management who led him to becoming a troubleshooter, and an assistant manager in Arizona, and then a general manager over construction." She smiled, "You can't start out at the top, but it can lead to your dream job."

Tourism Writing can help lead you to a career opportunity. It can help you learn to survive and deal with the public. That's what tourism is all about. Maybe Tourism Writing can prove Ms. Green's theory about how important it is when she said, "Hotels should put their highest paid people at the front desk," because you only get one chance to make a first impression."

Executive Director of Hancock County Chamber of Commerce Tish Williams said, "One thing needed as Tourism Director is to try to translate introductions to the city into more significant detail."

This was reinforced by her husband, George Williams, who once worked in the field of tourism in Mississippi and Maryland. He stressed that anything a community can do to entertain visitors and lengthen their stays is good. "The longer tourists visit, the more money they spend." More detailed comments by Williams are outlined in the chapter on Libraries.

Hancock County MS angel tree after Hurricane Katrina.

7
RESTAURANTS

Although locals who are regular customers keep many restaurants going, tourists also contribute to their success or failure. In any event, a restaurant's reputation is all important. Reviews quickly spread far and wide. The Dew Drop Inn in Mobile is a constant in a changing world. When former curb boy Jimmy Edgar, who was first a partner, then owned the restaurant for a short time, sold it to George Hamlin, his advice was "Don't change nothin'. You don't change the dining room or the help. Don't change the hot dog or nothin'." Hamlin didn't. Neither did his son Powell Hamlin when he took over the business. Booths have worn plaques with longtime customers' names on them and local artists' work still decorates the walls (dewdrop.mobile.weekly.com).

The success of the restaurant continued. Good food, good service, and reasonable prices keep drawing a crowd. As a plus, among the customers will probably be someone other Mobilians know, or diners may see native Mobilian Jimmy Buffet there, perhaps reminiscing about his visits as a child. Because of its appealing ambiance, the Dew Drop Inn has maintained its highly favorable status since it opened in 1924. This is also due to one item that is rarely forgotten once a customer has eaten it.

Every couple of months, an urge hits me. And it did one day a few weeks ago. I was hungry for a hot dog made famous by Mobile's oldest restaurant—the Dew Drop Inn, which is just seven years younger than the hundred year-old Chris' Hot Dogs in Montgomery, Alabama. I've eaten hot dogs all over the world, including in New York City, but none come close to the one made at the Dew Drop. Their nuclear red "dog" with their secret chili recipe, sauerkraut, ketchup, topped with one pickle on a steaming hot bun is something to die for. But I almost talked myself out of going to get one because it was close to noon and I knew all orange, Formica topped eighteen booths and seven tables would be occupied and the parking lot would be full. Still, my appetite won out.

In the pass-through from the kitchen, Powell Hamlin rapidly dished up orders. To my surprise, though, nobody was waiting at the checkout counter, so I placed my order and stepped aside. Seeing a stocky man approach with the words, "Hog breath is better than no breath at all," printed on his t-shirt, I suppressed a smile. He ordered a to-go and chatted with the cashier about his visit the day before. Then he pulled out a photo of a huge decorative bottle with *BEER* printed on it and turned to me. "Think you could drink all of that at one time?"

"I don't think so," I joked back. "I don't even like beer." I was reminded of a book by Lewis Grizzard. His doctor told him because of his heart condition, he could only have one glass of beer a day. So I made a reference to it and added, "Grizzard solved that problem," I tapped the large glass. "He found a glass like that. It held a gallon."

The man nodded as if he remembered that line and I pulled a business card out of my purse and handed it to him. "Since you like to read, this is my latest book."

He took a quick look. "Do you have any of these in your car?"

"Sure do."

"How much are they?"

"Hard backs are $33. They're numbered up to a hundred. And paperbacks are $20."

"I want a hard back." He chuckled. "Bet this will be the quickest sale you ever made."

We received our orders and went to my car. I took out a hard back copy of *George Wallace: An Enigma* and autographed it. Then I showed him my fantasy book—*Chance for Redemption.*

His eyes widened. "My sister's coming to Mobile soon and I bet she'd like that. How much is it?" I told him, he gave me the rest of the money he'd received in change, and added two dollars to pay for the book. Then he beamed a smile at me. "You're gonna hate this: I don't read. I'm dyslexic and the last book I read, *The Hobbit*, took me a year."

When he told me his parents had spent tons of money trying to fix his problem and said he didn't know how they managed to do that since they weren't rich, I was impressed with his appreciation of their efforts.

I didn't ask him to do a review on my books, but I did show him my e-mail address on the card and asked him to send me any comments he might have on the books. Hopefully, he'll tell his sister about the incident and she'll get a good impression of Mobile. Since he said he didn't read, maybe he'll let me know who gets both books and what they think about them. Or maybe our paths will never cross again. Still, even brief moments of shared friendship should be treasured. We should never miss a chance to spread good will. If he should come across a book using Tourism Writing later on, maybe he'll be inspired to make the effort to read it.

Perhaps others who walk through the door with a neon light streaming from a beer sign over it will discover the restaurant because of Tourism Writing. Powell Hamlin says, "While stories in magazines or information in hotels are good for business, a book with a permanent reference is much better. We have generations of local people coming here, but it's good for people from out of town to learn about our business. Tourists find it interesting."

He also commented that promoting courses in Tourism Writing could be "a big step in teaching writing." The affable owner sets the mood for the Dew Drop when he replies to people who say all he does is work. "It's not like work to me. I don't have to wear a coat and a tie. I love what I do. Every day is a joy." That could be a Tourism Writing story in itself.

Many visitors to the Gulf Coast can't wait to savor the type of food we're famous for in this area. If they leave the Dew Drop and drive west on Old Shell Road, dessert is waiting at Cammie's Old Dutch Ice Cream Shoppe. Since they make their own, it's a real treat. Also, the Pastry Shop isn't far away on Dauphin Street. They offer freshly made bakery products. Both are longtime business establishments.

Cammiesolddutch.com

To sample our seafood, locals in the know would probably suggest visiting Wintzell's Oyster House in the heart of downtown, a Mobile tradition since 1938. It's not only famous for its oysters and gumbo, but also for its signs covering the walls. One that's most amusing refers to this not being a fast food establishment and suggests if the service is too slow see the cashier: *Go to Helen Waite.* Another is philosophical; it says: *Circumstances do not make the man; they only reveal him to himself.* Those signs span a wide gap, from humor to philosophy, satire, and politics. The original owner, J.O. Wintzell, was well known for his dry sense of humor. One of his favorite sayings fit the definition of Tourism Writing by issuing a direct invitation to visit: "Come in and eat before we both starve."

Lots of business deals have been cut across the tables at this seafood restaurant. Many famous people have crossed this threshold. Photos on the wall show the former proprietor. Oliver Wintzell, standing next to well-known politicians, sports figures and those of almost any ilk or group you can think of. He could be a friend to all. Through the years, along with oyster-eating contests, Wintzell's has sponsored numerous worthy civic activities and charitable events such as Golf Tournaments and America's Young Woman of the Year (re-named Distinguished Young Women). This continues with the current owner. If you're from Mobile, the chances are good that you've dined here. If you haven't, whether you're a Mobilian or a visitor, maybe you'll be pleased if you give it a try.

wintzellsoysterhouse.com

#

Mobile can also brag about having a Ruth's Chris Steak House, a high-end restaurant. People often travel long distances to savor their sizzling steaks. In addition, T. P. Crockmier's, formerly a popular restaurant in midtown Mobile, now has a new building with a gorgeous interior featuring a circular staircase. It is a showplace in downtown Mobile. The owners, Bill Monahan and Mary Margaret Monahan are extremely proud that their regular customers followed them there.

Another well-frequented restaurant is Dick Russell's. It has plainer food, but lots of it. Famous for it's barbeque, many travelers know its location close to an I-10 exit. It is also well known for breakfast food, especially biscuits and homemade peach jam, pancakes and bacon. All food is freshly cooked and the service is prompt and efficient. People write rave reviews and they return for more of the tasty home cooking.

Florida can also brag about its food. In a quaint upstairs restaurant called Jelly Fish, opposite the beach on Perdido Key, FL, customers relax after a day in the sun. Neal Allison, floor manager, said the place was a partnership of two owners, and it could benefit from Tourism Writing because "We don't advertise much. Not many people know about us, most of our business comes from word of mouth. We don't use radio or billboards. Most of our business is from condos across the street." He felt that Tourism Writing advertisement would be very important.

"The unique thing about our restaurant is the variety on the menu. We offer steak, seafood, sushi, salad, and anything from filet to hamburgers."

He bragged that when Jimmy Buffet was at The Wharf, the next day he came to Jelly Fish. Allison smiled. "The owner called and arranged for Buffett to come in the back door. He was dressed like anyone else—slacks and a short sleeve shirt. The only people who knew we had a celebrity on the premises was the staff."

But Jimmy Buffett's presence proves one thing: If you have a reputation for fabulous food, you'll draw customers, even famous ones who have to sneak in to protect their privacy while they enjoy a good meal.

Even though all of these restaurants seem to prosper, you can't remain status quo in any business. It goes up, or down. So, all of them could benefit from being featured in Tourism Writing, whether it results in drawing new customers or encourages old customers who have drifted away to return. As politicians tell voters, "Say anything you like about me; just spell my name right." Name identification is crucial success.

Dew Drop Inn in Mobile, AL.

Wintzells Oyster House.

RESTAURANTS ❭ **63**

Jellyfish in Perdido Key, FL.

8
HISTORY

Chuck Torry, Research Historian of the City of Mobile, is well aware of the impact of tourism. He stated, "Mobile is no longer an industrial center. It lost its paper mills and needs to appeal to tourism. It's got to draw it in."

He referred to the time in 1870 when the city lost its charter and was dead broke. "They needed some way to bring in money, so they started the Carnival Court—with emperors, no queens." His shoulders straightened as he beamed with pride. "And look what that produced through the years. As the first city in the U.S. to have Mardi Gras, Mobile now enjoys the benefits of centuries of the income Mardi Gras produces—not just during the season, but year round.

"The spin-off is that float builders, hall rentals, sales and rental of formal wear for men and women, plus food and drink consumed, all add up to millions of dollars added to the economy. Tourists are part of the mix. Those who visit spend money on hotels and food, and no telling what else." He added, "And Tourism Writing can add to that benefit by drawing an even larger crowd to the event. Capitalizing on it should not be an option, it should be a given."

Gavin Schneider, Mobile History Museum's market and event coordinator, added other benefits. "Tourism writing helps us reach a different audience; the market is all commercial videos. People need a story to remember. In a story about Mardi Gras, people think of colors—other stories tell where you met your wife. Tourism Writing connects the story to the event." And people in Schneider's position can easily use Tourism Writing to add a new dimension by helping people *feel* what Mardi Gras is.

He said Tourism Writing can benefit the community in general because "People always look for a story to show others what a place is about. Mobile is not just as it is shown in films—it's much more and has a cultural history. People need to know the history and they can learn it by sharing stories of what happened in a city and what there is to do there. People tend to think of the south in terms of the Civil War era as being the flavor of it. Their emotions are tied to two hundred years ago—the past. That needs to change. Tourism Writing can show a great life and cut the negative outlook."

When more people are attracted to this area, they try the food and see the historic homes. Plus that, they experience "Southern hospitality" and feel "at home" enough to return, or maybe becoming interested in moving here.

To market Tourism Writing, Schneider suggested showing colleges the importance of the tourism industry and stressing that Tourism Writing is not a travel guide. "Emphasize the importance of it by using this book. Cities in the top twenty in commerce have a great tourism industry. It's necessary to understand venues—merchants who give little, get little—they need to participate to encourage tourism." He ended with an appealing benefit: "Tourist dollars spent lower citizens' taxes. Tourists pay taxes for you." Not many would argue that outside money helps. www.mobilehistorymuseum.com

But every visit to a place doesn't result in pleasant thoughts. Some memories aren't good. I recall one of mine that concerns a morose occurrence. It happened the only time I went to Demopolis, Alabama. A mentally challenged teenage girl's body was being pulled out of the Tombigbee River. Someone said she'd slipped off into it accidently. Others thought it was suicide.

Now, after reading PG Programs, in Alabama Power Company Magazine's January/Febuary 2017 issue, I'm getting a new, more positive impression of that city. It tells about points of attraction, painting a totally different picture from the distressing one embedded in my brain. Demopolis, from the Greek City of the People, has more there than this Tourism Writing has space to reveal. It appeals to my curiosity about this two hundred year-old, quaint town (13).

This small town of 7,500 residents, the gateway to the Black Warrior-Tombigbee Waterway boasts of having amenities of a big city. For example, they've had Christmas on the River for forty-five consecutive years. This one-day event features a nighttime water parade. The children's day parade has floats with paper and wood figures created by retirees and students, including a giant green and blue peacock nearly twenty-five feet tall. Volunteers number in the hundreds and up to 30,000 visitors arrive to attend the festivities.

Some of those visitors stay to take advantage of the opportunity to visit Gaineswood, one of America's top three Greek Revival homes or Bluff Hall overlooking the Tombigbee River. That 1850 two-story white frame antebellum Lyon Hall is thought to be the inspiration for the 1939 Broadway production of Lillian Hellman's *The Little Foxes* staring Tallulah Bankhead (from Alabama) and the 1941 movie starring Bette Davis.

Many people want to sample the homemade bread and cakes from Simply Delicious' Mennonite recipes. Others wait in long lines at the iconic farm building beside Highway 80 East. Inside The Red Barn, customers have to decide what to order from the long menu listing everything from chicken gizzards to steak and seafood. Longtime waitress Edna Brown chats with customers while she serves them, some "Miss Edna" has known for a very long time.

With its history and unique attractions, Demopolis not only has an intriguing past, it also has a present and a future. All appeal to visitors that will be welcomed with open arms.

9
PARKS

One of our greatest resources was preserved by our twenty-sixth president. After the passing of The Antiquities Act on June 7, 1906, Theodore Roosevelt, a conservationist, proclaimed places and objects of historic and scientific interest in federal ownership as national monuments. The National Park System administers those sites (History of the National Park System).

Fort Morgan and Fort Gaines are sites of one of the last battles of the Civil War, the Battle of Mobile Bay, which took place in the channel between Fort Morgan and Fort Gaines. During the confrontation, Rear Admiral David Farragut reportedly said, "Damn the torpedoes, full speed ahead!" In today's world, the ferry crossing that channel would be hard-pressed to follow his command.

In 1926, the U.S. sold Fort Gaines to the City of Mobile. The city gave the property to the Alabama Department of Conservation who deeded it to the Dauphin Island Park and Beach Board. Fort Morgan, maintained by the National Park Service, has been updated and is not like the original fort. On the other hand, Fort Gaines, still owned by the Dauphin Island Park and Beach Board, is preserved in its primitive state, the way it really was during the Civil War.

Another park full of history is managed by Mike Bunn, director of capital expansion and public affairs. Blakeley State Park at Spanish Fort, Alabama was also the site of a battle near the end of the Civil War. *Delta Explorer* boat tours and scenic nature cruises show visitors areas where battles were fought and Bunn is passionate about pointing out how Tourism Writing can help promote them.

He said, "Tourism Writing can help draw much-needed attention to cultural heritage resources such as parks, museums, and similar institutions which commonly struggle for exposure in our fast-paced and retail-oriented media outlets. But creative writing, involving historic sites and other tourism destinations, offers much more than the simple broadcasting of a name; when done well it can foster a special understanding of relevance to modern society and encourages a deeper engagement with the attraction of the public. These aspects are especially important to cultural heritage institutions today, as the travel and tourism world is increasingly more reliant on traveler expressions of the quality of their experiences than any self-generated marketing message."

That is certainly on target. We all get twenty-four hours a day. Each individual decides how to spend it—and his, or her, money.

"In checking on tourism destinations, travelers are likely to seek basic information on sites distributed by the sites and industry partners, "he said, "but they rely on traveler testimony in determining if a visit is worthy of their time. Tourism Writing can be thus critical in verifying essential messages that cultural heritage tourism destinations wish to communicate. This writing can also be instrumental in initiating new understandings of what the site has to offer and finding multiple meanings for the stories cultural heritage attractions tell."

One such story told of two schoolteachers who spent vacations touring Civil War sites each year. Discovering they had thirty-six hours to spend, they asked at a Mobile Bed and Breakfast about Spanish Fort. The owner said some of Spanish Fort and Blakeley had areas now occupied by a subdivision and suggested visiting Fort Gaines. He fixed them a box breakfast and gave them a list of places to visit—Bellingrath Gardens, Fort Gaines, the ferry to Fort Morgan, and return. But they didn't make it to all of those places. They arrived at Fort Gaines before seven a.m. and found it so intriguing that they didn't leave until it closed. It impressed them that it has reenactments of battles and the served the type of food used during the Civil War. These experienced Civil War buffs said, "It's the best preserved site we've ever seen." Since it is not under the National Park Service, its history is preserved.

Adding benefits to the community with Tourism Writing, Bunn continued, "Tourism Writing fosters a diversity of ways to appreciate cultural heritage resources, which can stimulate public discussion and contemplation of their importance to society as a sort of open dialogue. At its best, Tourism Writing can promote a unique sense of place by encouraging both understanding of and engagement with unique tourism venues that feature a cultural heritage focus. As this genre of literature has an inherently local focus, this aspect of its importance is especially significant in an increasingly global society."

In other words, if an emotional connection is established, a tourist forms a bond with a place or event and feels a need to investigate.

He also saw a need to market it effectively in order for schools to add it to their curriculum. "Tourism Writing is ideally suited to exposure in a variety of local public media such as newspapers and magazines, and of course in the ever-growing variety of social media platforms in full-length pieces, shorter blogs, and mentions in short posts," he said. "In addition, though, this writing should be featured at the venues under discussion as either a core component or ancillary resource in educational programming."

Bunn promotes events supporting writers. An *Alabama Authors' Day* was held at Blakeley last February. It featured brief presentations and discussions with several accomplished local authors who have recently published works based in Alabama's storied past.

Authors at this special event included:

Frye Gaillard, University of South Alabama Writer-in-Residence
Paula Webb, University of South Alabama Outreach Librarian
Brendan Kirby, Lifezette.com Senior Political Reporter
Mary S. Palmer, Faulkner University English Lecturer

Director of Membership of the Nature Conservancy Dave Strauss warns people about how important it is to protect threatened places "that provide us with everything from food and water to fresh air and the inspiration of its beauty." He states that 1.5 million acres of land are lost to development in the U.S. each year and he urges people to help save nature. For over sixty-five years, this organization has made significant and tangible progress by buying threatened land, convincing farmers and fishermen on sustainable practices and putting climate solutions into action. Strauss stresses that "the challenges facing our environment are complex…take one incredible powerful step to make sure we never reach a day when beautiful images are all we have left of our natural world" (Strauss). Perhaps Tourism Writing will be the medium to convince people to heed his warning.

GEORGE WALLACE: AN ENIGMA

The Complex Life of Alabama's Most Divisive and Controversial Governor

Mary S. Palmer

MOBILE UNDER SIEGE

Surviving the Union Blockade

PAULA LENOR WEBB

10
TRAVELING ACADEMICS: ADVANCED FORM OF TRAVEL TOURISM WRITING

by Paula Webb

Libraries, as spaces, need to continue to inspire the public to dream big and to think great thoughts. Cities, towns, and academic communities of all shapes and sizes need the free, open public spaces that libraries-and only libraries-provide.

(BiblioTech: Why Libraries Matter more than Ever in the Age of Google—John Palfrey)

INTRODUCTION

The dream of the great American journey has always rested in the back of our minds. If you live in the North, you may want to venture

South. If you live in the South, you may have ideas of venturing North or West. No matter where you travel, you will find one consistent thing: the library. In addition to public libraries, in many communities you may find a college or university library, a haven for those seeking to write professionally, particularly those who are in pursuit of Tourism Writing.

In a world full of Tripadvisors, Google Maps, and wonderful apps, gadgets and gizmos that help you achieve your lifelong dream to visit the Grand Canyon or New York City, why in the world would you visit a library? Why would you spend your valuable time traipsing through shelves of books? The academic library has a host of resources that go far beyond books and the capability of serving a wide range of research needs in one location.

What if I told you libraries today were more than books? What if I told you the role of a library and librarian is not so much about the books, but more about the people who use them? What if I told you there were great works of art in these libraries and rare collections that cannot be found anywhere else?

Journey with me through this book chapter as I share with you the value of academic libraries and their impact on Tourism Writing.

AS A SERVICE

One day recently, a man walked into the Marx Library at the University of South Alabama and came up to the Reference desk and asked me a simple question, "Do I have to reserve a study room?" He took me a bit by surprise. This gentleman was distinguished and in his later years. He was not like the young bright-eyed, fresh faces I see everyday.

As a Librarian, I have the privilege to ask questions to find out more information; besides, I couldn't resist. I asked, "Would you mind telling me what you are working on so I can help you better?" I hoped it would be good, and it was.

He said, "No problem. I am in town researching my early family history for a book. All ties bring me back to Mobile, Alabama."

I was excited, not only was he here to visit all of our wonderful libraries and collections throughout the city, but he was using the wealth of resources our university library had available. I was quick to tell him what we had to offer a traveling researcher to help him have a positive and successful visit to Mobile, Alabama.

What did this patron know about academic libraries many others who are practicing Tourism Writing do not? Most university and college libraries are open to the public. If an academic library is a part of the Federal Depository Library Program, by law it must have the facilities available to the public. Academic libraries tend to be in larger buildings than public libraries and there are usually study spaces designed specifically for those who are committed to serious research. There are academic libraries that have quiet space you can use for a period of time. In addition, there are designated quiet study spaces in most academic libraries.

To facilitate research you need certain vital elements: some colleges or universities provide reliable WiFi services, comfortable furniture, and a handy place to purchase copious amount of caffeine. If you forgot your laptop, some university libraries provide computers open to the public, usually loaded with all the software you can use to write, such as Microsoft Word. These libraries try to meet the needs of the students attending the university; your access to the same benefits in the library is a perk.

When you begin your writing about the location you are touring, you may need background information to support your literary work. Local books and newspapers, as well as databases and electronic journals can be found in academic libraries. A university campus is full of researchers learning more about their environment and they need tools to do their job well. If you are writing about a local attraction, chances are good professors will have students visit and write about local attractions for course work. Academic libraries often make it a point to purchase and have materials available for these students.

Many academic librarians are interested in local history and attractions and have assisted students and other researchers in locating local and regional information. They tend to research tourist locations before visiting to fully enjoy the experience of the attraction. Mobile, Alabama, for example, is a very old city with a fascinating history. Years ago, I toured Oakleigh House, an antebellum mansion in downtown Mobile. I was so amazed at what I learned during the tour that I soon volunteered at their Minnie Mitchell Archives. My experience working there inspired me to write a book about the city. My book, *Mobile Under Siege: Surviving the Union Blockade*, was published by History Press in 2016 and since that time, I have had many people visit the library and inquire about my research and other resources in Mobile.

AS A DESTINATION

Academic libraries can not only be a huge asset to those conducting research, they can also be a travel destination. Academic libraries have a long history of being a place people or organizations donate family heirlooms, special collections, or their personal research. If a donor of the collection adds additional funds, then the academic library can be the best location to house and maintain the collection for many generations to come. The library has the ability to hire professionals to assess the collection, staff to maintain the collection, and the ability to promote the collection to the community.

A prime example of this is the John Grisham Room at Mississippi State University. "The John Grisham Room is a beautifully appointed room, exhibit area and conference suite on the third floor of the Mitchell Memorial Library. Its main purpose is to provide a place where people may view materials and memorabilia from the writings and achievements of bestselling author, former Mississippi legislator (1983–1990), and MSU alumnus John Grisham" (http://lib.msstate.edu/grisham). When you realize how challenging it could be for Grisham to keep track of all of his manuscript materials and notes from his research, it only makes sense for him to find a better way of maintaining all this information.

Academic libraries often display donated materials and other resources in creative and engaging ways. The library where I work is a perfect example. One donor was very fond of Mark Twain, so he requested a study room be named for this author. The room is complete with a portrait and the library maintains books in the collection to further study about the author. In another part of the building, there is an etching made by Rembrandt in 1634 entitled "The Angel Appearing to the Shepherds." The etching was a gift from the University of South Alabama class of 1968.

People have travelled to various locations for years, writing about their journey, what they experienced while they visited the location, and how it changed their life. In a similar way, when a professor is writing a peer-reviewed research article, dissertation or a book, he, or she, may travel to access materials for the project. Traveling professors may stay at a local hotel, eat at local restaurants, and visit local libraries to gather information for their research project. Whether professors realize this or not, they are participating in Tourism Writing.

I recently met with Deborah Gurt, assistant librarian and digital processing archivist at the McCall Rare Book and Manuscript Library at the University of South Alabama, to get her input regarding those who visit her library. The McCall Library contains numerous collections including photographs, manuscripts and rare books.

When Ms. Gurt was asked the role of academic libraries in travel tourism, she stated, "It is not at all obvious that there would be a link between these two things, but in fact, we do occasionally get visitors who come from out of town specifically to use our collections. We recently had a scholar come from out of state with two students and they stayed for two weeks working with a manuscript collection for historical research. If I had to generalize, the largest groups of users of our collections fall into two groups: historians like the one I mentioned doing scholarly work, and family researchers. These two populations represent both professional archive users and informal users, who are occasionally as skilled as the professionals at navigating collections and extracting the information they seek."

Ms. Girt continued to explain, "The purpose of the archives is simple: to document and preserve records of the past, with a focus on the Alabama Black Belt Region, the area surrounding the university and the University of South Alabama, specifically. The McCall Library sees its purpose to provide access to evidence of the lives and activities of the people who came before us." Ms. Gurt sees it as her job "to make sure that the collections represent a wide variety of voices, and that they are organized in ways that make sense and are user-friendly for experienced researchers as well as novices."

I earlier mentioned how the academic library is designed to cover a wide range of material interesting to the tourism writer within one location. This concept transfers to the historical collections maintained at the McCall Library. Ms. Gurt told me, "One of the really interesting things about the archives is they represent and demonstrate the diversity of Mobile, Alabama. They have records of social clubs (German Relief Association, and Howard Lodge Collection to name a couple) which drew on people from all walks of life who chose to spend their free time together. They also have collections representing groups who had an impact on Mobile's development, MOWA Choctaw Indians, the Jewish community, African American leaders, all of whose voices can be found in the archives."

AS COURSEWORK

The academic library can also play a role in the lives of those who are seeking a career in the travel tourism industry. I met with the University of South Alabama's Interim Chair of Hospitality and Tourism Management, Dr. Evelyn K. Green, who took the time to explain how the academic library can really help those who are seeking a degree in this program. She shared her definition of a tourist, "Anytime someone travels fifty miles and beyond they are considered a tourist. They are doing touristy stuff, including educational tourism." If we take this definition and add in the element of Tourism Writing, then the concept can be utilized for those students who are practitioners seeking a career in tourism management.

An example of what her students are working towards can be found on the course website, "Hospitality and Tourism Management (HTM) covers a broad spectrum of business sectors within the service industry. The HTM program offers an interdisciplinary perspective that prepares students for local and global hospitality and tourism careers. Students participate in academic, observational, situational, and experiential settings to meet program competency requirements in operation and service management, financial and human resource management, global leadership, and personal and professional career development." (https://www.southalabama.edu/colleges/ceps/htm/)

In each of these stages, Tourism Writing can be a valuable part of preparing them for this growing industry.

The academic library is also able to help those students who are a majoring in travel tourism and have to participate in the public relations plans for their future place of employment. They will be required to do such things as research, compose and distribute press releases and feature stories. They may help with hosting travel writer conferences, group writing tours or individuals traveling to work on their latest project. They may also help with the ongoing and development and maintenance of written communications and the placement of those communications in certain professional outlets. Dr. Green suggested, "The library could maintain a collection of print and online travel guides and other various types of travel information my students could use while preparing for their careers. Let's say they want to travel to the Netherlands for work. Instead of going to a bookstore and getting one of those little travel books, the library could have a collection of those books available on line for them to use wherever they are in the world. It would be good to know there is a repository of this kind of information the students could access at anytime."

Travel tourism, writing about the journey and academic libraries can work together as students and others utilize library resources as they work to become experts in their various fields.

CONCLUSION

Travel Tourism Writing and academic libraries really do work together in various and unexpected ways. Naturalist Andrew James Pritchard said, "Besides, by traveling to all corners of the globe it allows me to future define the ever-changing world we live in, which in turn helps me to redefine myself, therefore it is an important process towards becoming a complete person" (Andrew James Pritchard, The Man in Seat 11B). If we successfully utilize academic libraries and how they complement and support travel tourism writers, then the writings produced from their journey can also be much more complete.

11
POLITICIANS

People in the political arena are involved in everything that goes on in their city, county, state and even in Washington, D.C. Their hands have to be on the pulse of the nation. Although their own territories are their main concern, they are affected by what goes on at every level of government. What happens in Washington, D.C. trickles down to places like Tishomingo, MS, (Population 1,200) or Clio, Alabama (Population 1,000).

Politics rules our lives. The more aware of this we are, the more we realize the importance of voting. This came home to me once when I was campaigning for a presidential candidate and I asked a co-worker to vote for him. A week later, she walked in the office flashing a smile. "I voted for your candidate," she said.

With a wrinkled brow, I asked, "How did you do that? The election isn't till November."

She shook her finger at me. "Oh, you're wrong. I went home this weekend and his name was on the ballot."

Sucking in my cheek, I suppressed a smile. Seems like a candidate running for some local office in her small hometown in North Alabama was a beneficiary of my campaigning. My fault for not being clearer. How did I go wrong? Maybe if we'd had some Tourism Writing back then, she'd have learned more about researching candidates before voting. Maybe not.

There are many ways to learn about voting. In researching for another book, a biography of George Wallace entitled, *George Wallace: An Enigma*, I had the opportunity to take a trip on a presidential campaign. It gave me a chance to see the inner workings of a political campaign. As an objective observer, my evaluation was that some of it was organized; some was not. For one thing, when we left Mobile for North Carolina, volunteers weren't sure whether their expenses would be paid. On the trail, while the people in charge understood "having a hall too small" made a rally appear to be well attended, so they booked one for this appearance, choosing sites to campaign seemed haphazard. Often, too, they failed to get permits to solicit. Workers felt uneasy passing out pamphlets at malls and weren't as aggressive as they would have been otherwise. Still, because of the volunteers and leaders enthusiasm and the candidate's dynamic speech, the trip seemed to be a success. The volunteers' expenses were paid. However, the campaign failed; his opponent was elected president.

While the executive level is the highest-ranking office in the United States, leadership starts on the lower steps of the ladder, in communities. For example, members of city councils have a huge impact on what happens in a city. If they do their job properly, they represent all of the people they serve. One councilman in our area understands this very well. His attitude was clear in an interview.

Mobile's most well known City Councilman Fred Richardson's ready smile was welcoming. Born in Nymph, Alabama as one of twelve children, he is familiar with hardship. This was especially true after his father—a cook, a moonshiner, and a farmer—died at age forty-nine. Although he paid tribute to his birthplace—also the birthplace of his brother Shelton, once Mayor of North Randall, Ohio, and of Moddie D. Taylor who helped make the atom bomb—by having a sign erected on Interstate 65 at Exit 83 directing people to Nymph, he is also dedicated to promoting the city he serves—Mobile. Broad-minded, he supports people of all persuasions and ethnic groups. "If you're a member of the Klan and you call for Fred Richardson, if you ring, I will spring. I will represent every person in District One," he said on WKRG-TV June 12, 2017, using a wit that makes him a highlight of council meetings.

It is obvious that this councilman loves his city. He bragged, "We have a lot to celebrate in Mobile and we haven't done a good job selling it to our own citizens. Foreigners, yes, we've sold them on our city. But Mobilians are often quick to talk down our city. It's partly because they don't *know* what we have here. We need to have writing about tourism and give people here in-depth knowledge about what we have to offer. Our citizens need to know." With a sigh, he added, "Politicians condemn the city. They mention crime and bring out the worst, hoping promises to fix the problems will get them elected." His eyes lit up. "People also say there's nothing to do in Mobile because they don't know what's available. What you're doing will help."

Richardson has a very good record of promoting the city at conventions, proving the interesting fact that Mobile is a blend of cultures, a city that has lived under five different flags. "Mobile needs to embrace all of history," he said. "Nowadays, we have plenty to offer, such as thirteen blocks of an entertainment district downtown. We also have some little known historical buildings such as the Stone Street Baptist Church, the oldest in Alabama." He cited a need on Interstate 10 for a sign letting visitors know of its existence.

The Moon Pie Drop on New Year's Eve is another attraction that no doubt led to the establishment of a MoonPie General Store in Mobile. Richardson, who is involved with Alabama's upcoming Bicentennial Celebration, expressed enthusiasm that having courses in Tourism Writing would greatly benefit Mobile and Alabama. www.moonpiegeneralstore

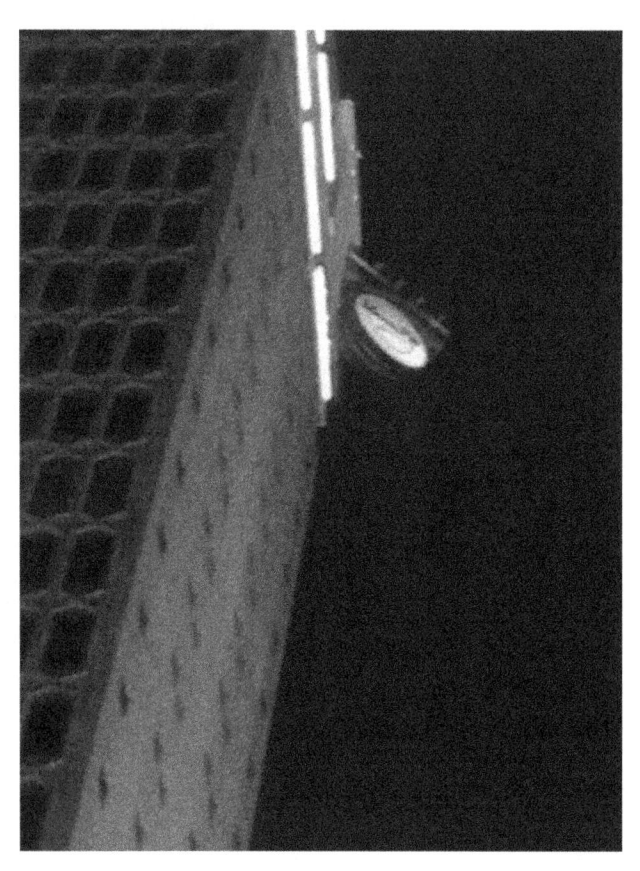

Moon Pie Drop in Mobile, AL.

Stone Street Baptist Church.

12
REAL ESTATE

Wendy James, who deals in real estate in addition to running the Kate Shepard House Bed and Breakfast, said Tourism Writing could benefit people in that profession, too. She sells new homes, but living in an old Victorian home taught her to recognize the beauty of older houses and she understands the need to preserve them.

She expressed her feelings by saying, "I like to brag that we are the most published house in Mobile. We are well known for our 1897 architecture and we are listed in several architecture publications not just in Alabama but across the country. At least a half a dozen artists have beautifully recreated our house and we continue to stumble across more in stores. Kate Shepard, her outstanding reputation and the school named after her makes the locals aware of her family home. Our bed and breakfast has received accolades and editorials for over 14 years. Our Pecan Praline French Toast continues to be listed on the state of Alabama's "100 dishes to eat before you die". Last but not least, the historic papers left in our attic have attracted national and international attention."

As a realtor, she feels that any time you find a way to bring new people to an area, you're bringing in potential clients, people who need a place to live.

It's interesting to note that houses half a century ago sold for one-fifth of the price of those same older houses currently back on the market, or newer ones of comparable size and amenities. Even allowing for inflation and the offset of higher incomes, that's a huge increase. Despite the cost, in today's world, homebuyers tend to seek more elaborate housing than they did in the past, including first time purchasers.

Higher costs mean higher sales' commissions. That's a plus. So is information about areas provided by Tourism Writing, which gives people the opportunity to make the best choice possible when buying a home. It has another beneficial effect: Tourism Writing generates citizens' pride in the community. And pride leads to progress.

A former real estate agent, Joyce Bowers, said when she dealt with out-of-town customers while driving them around Mobile, "They immediately commented on the beauty of the trees, the waterways, buildings with ironwork, and old antebellum and Victorian homes."

This Mobilian learned to appreciate her birthplace. "When I left Mobile and lived in Florida, I realized how much I took for granted. When I returned, I vowed never to leave again." She laughed. "But we won't talk about the humidity problem. Every place has something."

One incident she experienced amused her. "I had a call from a Secret Service guy and didn't feel comfortable showing him around since he wanted to go into remote places down dirt roads looking for a house. So I had a friend go with me and she sat in the back seat and I sat in the front. Come to find out, when his wife came to town, she told me, 'I have breast cancer and I'm coming to Mobile so my sister can help me with the children.'" Bowers shrugged. "You never know what will happen. They ended up buying a house on a main thoroughfare full of traffic, not out in the country."

13
CEMETERIES

During his twenty-two years on the job, Tighe Marston has not had one single complaint from the people he cares for daily. Day after day silence prevails as he walks among them, but they tell their stories without saying a word.

The last place anybody goes has a wealth of history, much of it is inscribed on tombstones. Consequently, Magnolia Cemetery, established in 1836, offers many opportunities for creative writing. Municipal Cemeteries Manager for the City of Mobile Marston, said, "It offers students a chance to obtain ideas, such as Eagle Scout projects. They can see things in history and picture the story about the event." He mentioned that they have a free public tour in November. "We'll do a group tour anytime with from five to thirty people from October 1 until March 31." Eager to promote this historic site, Marston is also available for presentations to organizations.

The historic landmark, which has always been owned by Mobile, is under the Department of Parks and Recreation and Marston is the only city employee. The building is owned by the Department of

Veteran Affairs. Although they have not used the building since 1970, they take care of the outside. Friends of Magnolia Cemetery lease it for a minimal amount and they take care of the inside.

Many points can be made by Tourism Writing; for example, the marker says there are 50,000 graves but 100,000 plus graves are actually in the cemetery's 160 acres. Marston also spoke of Church Street Cemetery being the oldest in the city and cited some little known facts. "It dates back to 1820. When it was established Mobile's population was eighty percent Catholic, so one-third of the cemetery was reserved for Catholics, one-third was for Masons, and one-third for protestants. In the yellow fever epidemic, two hundred and forty five people were buried in two months. Some victims in Campo Santo Cathedral Square were moved to Church Street. They moved the *known* burials, but they missed some." And it seems they've found parts of bodies since then on the site.

Marston also pointed out, "The first things a city needs are food, shelter and a burial place." His next statement was amusing. "The leaky atrium in Mobile's Government building was the site of the first cemetery outside the fort when Mobile was founded in 1702."

In comparing two of Mobile's cemeteries, Marston said, "Magnolia is prettier than Church Street." He elaborated how more decorative statues in Magnolia Cemetery compared to plainer ones in the Church Street Graveyard. "In the Victorian era, gravesites were predominantly considered places of temporary sleep. For example, a child on a death couch is turned on its side to look asleep, waiting to arise. And the structure of the cover of the grave is like a bed—with a headboard, footboard and side rails. They dropped parts and now headstones carry the only asleep motif."

He mentioned how terminology referring to places arranging for burial had changed. "It went from Undertaker Parlor, to

Mortuary, to Funeral Home, to Final Arrangements Center and now it's called a Crematorium or Multi Purpose Memorial Center—using semantics for a softer sound."

Pointing out how other things evolved, he said, "They used to bury people fast because of deterioration. When I first started working in this business, I once wanted to pinch a guy who died at eight a.m. and was buried at three p.m. I wondered if he was still alive."

He referred to how Tourism Writing could show "This is what Mobile was like a hundred years ago. It shows the type life doctors, lawyers, farmers or others lived. People then had a death cult; they were fascinated with death. You can see it in the fancy coffins or jewelry and sculptures. With embalming coming in 1840, using arsenic, bodies could be held a week." He told of a bell listener who stayed by the grave a few days to be sure the person was dead, and of the stoic Victorians who allowed no crying. Sometimes relatives who feared they'd break down did not attend their loved-one's funeral. He also mentioned iron cages being used to stop body snatchers. He spoke of changes, saying, "We have changed our traditions. Now there's generally no wake the night before burial, maybe no church ceremony, only a memorial service."

One of their most common problems is theft. He told of more than one incident of people stealing flowers from graves, oftentimes taking them home. "I saw a lady put flowers in the trunk of her car. When I confronted her, she said she didn't like them on her mother's grave. When she kept arguing, I told her, 'They're not yours. I'll call the police.'" He shook his head. "She was nicely dressed and had a nice car. But she didn't mind telling me, 'I'm not stealing them. They won't leave the cemetery. I'm just going to move them.'"

One Monday after Easter, he had another such incident. "Two sweet, gray-haired ladies had a station wagon full to the roof with Easter lilies and they were driving out of the cemetery. I knew a faster way to cut them off. When I stopped them, one shrugged and explained, 'I'm going to take them home and plant them. Easter's over; they have no use to those people.'

"When I said, 'You didn't buy them,' she looked at those 400 lilies and started crying. I took the lilies to my office and when anyone came by saying someone had stolen some, I let them take their pick."

Two bizarre incidents involved someone doing genealogy research. "This lady in her twenties came in to research saying she wanted her grandmother's records," Marston said. "She was really upset when I asked for the woman's name. 'You're the records' keeper,' she said, 'You should know her name.' When she stomped out, all I could think of was, 'cemetery stupid.'"

The second incident was at a graveside service. "Signs directing cars started at the gate and were placed all the way to the site itself," Marston said. "When the service was almost over a lady pulled up blocking the line of cars. She was well dressed and her hair was done. She jumped out of the car, cursing me with language I never heard from merchant seamen in my family. 'I couldn't tell which way to go,' she yelled. 'You made me miss my friend's funeral.'

"I told her I was terribly sorry, but I had signs. She stomped her foot. 'I saw the sign and the first sign pointed up. How the hell can I go up?'"

Dealing with grief-stricken survivors is a solemn business requiring diplomacy, sensitivity and even restraint in ludicrous situations. However, if you don't laugh, you'll cry, so seeing the humorous side of things can lighten those burdens.

Marston gets no arguments from the dead, but the living he has to deal with make up for it with outrageous occurrences and illogical back talk. All are good fodder for Tourism Writing. www.magnoliacemetery

CEMETERIES › **99**

Church Street Graveyard.

Foggy scene in Magnolia Cemetery.

Magnolia Cemetery Night Scene.

14
POLICE

Mobile Police Chief Lawrence Battiste, who has been on the job four months, also does mentoring for a Boys and Girls Leadership Program at Strickland Youth Center. He feels that those youth can benefit from Tourism Writing. "It may lead them to understand and learn the culture of Mobile," he said. "They don't always know much about the city they grew up in. Young men who learn about places like Austal discover they can go into welding." Such an opportunity may result in a better life for those young people.

Battiste, whose daughter was an Azalea Trail Maid, felt young girls could be helped to mature by taking part in such activities, "By being exposed to different cultures, they discover there's more to life. They can get to know people and to seek new adventures."

With a son following in his footsteps as a police officer, he understood that Tourism Writing could engage youth in research, which offers opportunities to see how others live. "They go to unfamiliar neighborhoods and discover people live in different size homes and drive types of cars." Despite that, he felt we have more in common than we realize. But he saw the need to use tools like Tourism Writing to "help youth traumatized by experiences—to take them out of that environment and show them something to work toward. We should not just *tell* them about what's available, we should let them observe it—give them hope for a better future."

He did add that mentoring wasn't always easy. One day, he was very tired and almost ready to stop. "I was wondering if it was worth volunteering. The young men were forced to be there and I didn't think they were paying attention."

Finally, he asked the group, "Are you getting anything out of this?"

"'Chief,'" one replied, "'you show up; we get something.'"

Convinced that if you touch just one, your effort is worth-while, he was motivated and continued mentoring.

#

Former Marine and Mobile Chief of Police, James Barber, now holds the position of Executive Director of Public Safety for the City of Mobile. This man—who calls himself an "Army brat," because his father was in the military—says Tourism Writing is beneficial because "It allows people to learn about Mobile's rich history. As a marketing factor, when you increase tourism, you increase job opportunities and if you put young people to work, they serve the community. That gets them off the streets." Consequently, the city is safer.

He spoke about crimes and how and why they occur. "It's easier to get a gun than a job." And he mentioned, "Police who got heavily involved with young people realized they have no role models." He suggested to young men, "Pull your pants up or nobody will want to hire you." Then he added, "Not all are college material; some need vocational training."

He said Public Service Director Chris Murphy once asked him if he had a choice to use money to improve downtown or hire 100 new police officers which one would he choose. "I told him 'downtown' because I've watched Mobile grow and with a viable downtown you have less problems." He spoke of the past when Mobile's downtown was all but deserted and crimes were rampant. Now, they are more unusual in that area, so they get a lot of press when one occurs. More people; less problems.

One case Barber was involved with as a young detective was a murder near the University of South Alabama. The shooting occurred when a student, a Wiccan named Jamie Kellam Letson, stalked Kathleen Foster and lured her into the woods to shoot her. Both were USA students from Pascagoula, MS. Although the murder took place in 1980, Letson was not tried and convicted until 2010, thirty years after the crime. Jealousy was cited as the motive.

But that tragedy has a recent twist with an amazing result. Jamie Letson's daughter is not following in her mother's footsteps. Meagan Letson overcame struggles and challenges of her mother being in and out of jail and her dad abandoning her. She lived with her maternal grandmother and step-grandfather from the time she was one year old. Ronald and Fay Milton adopted her and her sister when she was eight years old. The up-shoot is that in 2012, Meagan overcame adversity to be one of 104 students across the country named a Horatio Alger National Scholar. This $20,000 award will help her in her goal to attend medical school to be a general surgeon.

Ronald Milton realizes Meagan "has a lot of scarring...She won't talk about it...But you can tell the hurt was there." Like roses that need rain to bloom, Meagan needed nurturing. Apparently that need was filled by her grandmother and step-grandfather.

The Horatio Alger Association formed in 1947 "to dispel the belief among the nation's youths that the American dream was no longer attainable," seems to have reached its goal in Meagan Letson's case (Ruddiman, Susan, *The Mississippi Press*, February 10, 2012 at 7:14 a.m.). If finding a way out of a horrendous situation by learning about opportunities from the printed word helped Meagan, it can help many others. It just has to be made available to them.

Barber knows the value of giving youth chances. This man who came up through the ranks understands the need for police officers to know modern police tactics. "The environment has changed," he said. "At schools, we used to practice fire drills, now we practice terrorist drills. It's a big challenge. First, we had criminal threats; in 2001, the criminal threat was national security; in the past three years, the general public is threatened. Today, violence shares the headlines with other threats."

He feels all of this is due to political change, religious change, and social change. "Kids today play games with the goal of beating the record, being the high scorer." He felt children are being "desensitized" when practicing shooting playing games. This leads to loss of respect for life.

On another level, he spoke of motives of terrorists saying, "They think by inflicting mass casualties they'll give people the feeling that government can't protect you." But he showed hope. "The upside is that they are alienating the general public."

Maybe Tourism Writing can cause readers to take heed and beware.

15

MILITARY

Tourism Writing ranks high in its ability to help people serving in the military who are frequently transferred from one base to another. If they are provided with information about their new location, it will most likely be general, such as travel guides. It's unlikely that it will include things like a house in Stockton, AL built by hand by a returning Confederate soldier and later occupied by Colonel Dorris Smith (U.S. Air Force Retired) who raised emus and sold them and their byproducts until his death. Around the corner is a restaurant called the Stagecoach, frequented mostly by locals, but it is sought out by some visitors.

Nor are such guides prone to listing places like the McGehee Farm, in Kushla, Alabama, even though one of the final treaties ending the Civil War was signed there. Unfortunately, it is not currently open to the public. They might also omit Biloxi, MS's Mary Mahoney's Restaurant and its garden's 2,000 year-old sprawling oak tree called the Patriarch which survived numberless hurricanes. Even if some of these are mentioned, they may not be described in a way to appeal to tourists enough to make them want to visit. Oftentimes, it's the story behind the story that creates interest.

It is a given that Tourism Writing affects young people. Lieutenant Colonel John Schluter (USAF Retired) of Bossier City, LA understands this and sees a way to capitalize on it. He said, "Since many people know they will be joining the military before graduating college, having a degree program that could complement their prospective travel could be enticing. As most servicemen and women travel to many places throughout the world for temporary duty (TDY), tourism writing could allow people in the military an opportunity to earn supplemental income by writing about their experiences. In addition, most servicemen and women also are moved every couple of years. This experience would also provide unique insights to writing about different locations, which could be quite different from those traveling for leisure only." It's a viable new possibility to encourage writers.

Schluter also felt Tourism Writing could benefit the community in general in much the same way. "As with the military," he said, "those who travel a lot could find usefulness in tourism writing… especially if they want to combine travel with their work. A tourism writing program would provide prospective writers with the tools necessary to perform this unique style of writing."

In commenting about the best way to market Tourism Writing to schools, he replied, "This is a tough question. I think my suggestion is to market as not only a major degree program, but as a minor degree program. First, you would have to show universities that there is a requirement for this program. Secondly, you would have to show them what the job market looks like for a person with these skill sets. If there is truly a market, you need to get information from these employers as to what types of skill one would need to be a tourism writer." His on-target observations are worth consideration.

A female who served in the military has a different approach to Tourism Writing.

After entering the U.S. Marine Corps at age eighteen, Judith Jacob experienced many things in her two-year hitch. She said she "loved every minute of it. We are a family." During a very sad time, her military associates consoled her. "When my daughter died, I was a civilian, but Navy and Air Guard folks came to her memorial."

A good event was meeting the man she married. "I met my husband in Germany. We deployed for 15 days and I noticed him on the plane going there. We always seemed to run into each other while there. We married a year later. These thoughts are my favorite memories of the military."

Fifteen years after being active, she joined the Tennessee Air National Guard and stayed twenty-two years, retiring with a total of twenty-four years military. Parttime military personnel are affected by Tourism Writing, too. Judith F. Jacob, NFG USAF 164 MSG (Retired), Memphis, TN, testifies to this. "As a former guardsman," she said, "I can say we do deploy to Alabama, Louisiana, and surrounding states. While deployed, we always look for new and different places to visit, so we can learn about those places and enjoy them. Yes, your book would be valuable to military. National guardsmen, army as well as reservists, also deploy and want to enjoy the places they go."

She explained that they are not transferred around but only deploy for a couple of weeks. Since their time in any location is limited, Tourism Writing could help them plan activities in advance;

by reading ahead, servicemen and women will already know what interests them in a certain area before they reach their destination. "We look at the places we're deployed to for family-oriented sites," she added. "This may include planning future return trips if people like what they see. We are always looking for new and different places to take our families for vacation." Tourism Writing can provide information to fill that slot.

16
MUSEUMS

Director of the Mobile Mardi Gras Trail, Ann Pond, sees several ways Tourism Writing could benefit her group. The trail is marked with bricks commemorating people and organizations and it leads followers down past routes taken by Mobile Mardi Crews from the time Mobile began celebrating the event with parades—the first city to do so in the United States.

Pond said, "There's a huge trend today to tell real stories about people. That's what we want the Mardi Gras Trail to do. By attending walking tours they can learn about architecture. This trail is the only one in Mobile showing what the city is like, how we live. Tourism Writing can help by livening up history.

"It can also help if we could connect the Moon Pie and use tiny ones strategically placed around town as a logo. Tourism could have a theme which sticks in people's minds when they leave Mobile."

She's right. If these things could be worked into Tourism Writing courses, it would get the word out and tweak people's curiosity.

Readers would tell their friends and more tourists would pour into Mobile, enjoying our amenities and spending money to help pay our taxes.

On the same route the first Mardi Gras Parades took, a new business is attracting a lot of attention. In addition to appealing to tourists, the MoonPie Shop has introduced its employees to the uniqueness of Mobile.

When asked how someone in his occupation could benefit from Tourism Writing, Assistant Manager of the MoonPie Shop said, "Anything that spreads awareness of the area is a boon to industries like MoonPie." Wes Smith, from Chattanooga, Tennessee, said he loves Mobile's history. "It's a hundred years older than Chattanooga and has an old world feel about it. It's different."

His first Mardi Gras appalled him. "I've never seen anything like it. It struck me that the whole city poured out for one huge party." He grinned. "I got hit with three sets of beads and a few Moon Pies, but I didn't mind that."

But one thing was a mystery to him. "The first night I went to a parade, my friend was hit in the chest with a Moon Pie. He snatched up, unwrapped and bit into it. It was orange, a flavor the company had discontinued making. And it was fresh. Mystified, I called our Chattanooga Bakery and they assured me no special orders were produced and no new orange Moon Pies were being made."

He scratched his head. "I know it was ours, too. I checked the label. I also heard other people say they caught those orange Moon Pies at different parades. I can't figure it out."

It might not be a complete mystery. The possible answer is that some revelers froze those pies and defrosted them, refreshing them before tossing them from floats to people on the street clapping and screaming, "Moon Pie! Moon Pie! Moon Pie!"

One photo of that to accompany Tourism Writing makes a deep impression on readers. It appeals to their desire to come to Mobile to enjoy the festivities and be a part of a celebration that makes people so happy.

The Executive Director of the Mobile Medical Museum Daryn Glassbrook, a graduate of Purdue University, didn't start his career in that field. He first was involved in art, and then wrote grants before ending up working for a non-profit organization. However, he sees a connection where art and science both are means of investigation.

"In the early history of science," he said, "we used to see the arts and science as two separate things. But the study of anatomy is drawn from the best anatomical figures. Artists in the Renaissance became anatomists by attempting to create lifelike sculptures of the human figure. Artists and anatomists worked together to investigate the body through dissection. Art led to anatomy." He also stressed that both science and art are important. They overlap. Both are a means of investigation. Both involve ideas, theories, and hypotheses that are tested in places where mind and hand come together—the laboratory and studio. Daryn pointed out that artists, like scientists, study—materials, people, culture, history, religion, mythology—and learn to transform information into something else. In ancient Greece, the word for art was *lachne*, from which *technique* and *technology* are derived—terms that are aptly applied to both scientific and artistic practices.

Housed in the Vincent Doan Walsh House, Mobile's oldest private residence still standing in its original location, this museum features everything from an iron lung, to an ancient dentist's chair, to a collection of false teeth and old eyeglasses. In addition, two

1869 larger than life paper mache anatomical models from Paris are probably the museum's most unusual feature. They were completely restored to the tune of $50,000. Dr. Josiah Clark Nott, Mobile Medical School's founder used them. Few museums have such models that were used before X-rays. They show inner organs, blood vessels, the heart and the intestines. The lymphatic system is colored green. In the past, professors of anatomy used them to illustrate their lectures.

How could Tourism Writing benefit this type of museum? Glassbrook said, "It could interest more visitors. It's a teaching museum, not only for local medical students but for other students in the community." He added, "The history of medicine has general interest. It touches on many aspects. It's fascinating to learn about how Mobile changed in health care through the years." He said most of their customers are from out of town. "They come from all over the world, Poland, Australia. They find us through Trip Advisor, Visit Mobile, our website, and word-of-mouth. They explore our great culture."

Glassbrook understands that people outside of the medical field can't look at a fact sheet and absorb the significance or history of objects. So, he turns the facts into narratives using the vernacular and makes the history come to life. "Young people get into the past and figure out what it means to them. It helps them understand what we have now that people didn't have then. Or what they had then that we no longer have. I don't want them to leave with the impression that people then were dumb. They don't deserve to be criticized. They made mistakes; we all do. But the observations of some of those people led to breakthroughs. For example, in 1798, Edward Jenner discovered the small pox vaccine after overhearing two milkmaids talking about cow pox." Tourism Writing could add to this type of knowledge.

As to why Tourism Writing is important, Glassbrook said they recently had a history-writing contest. Sixth graders visited the museum, took the tour, and chose an object to write about, such as the iron lung. They had a cash prize and each participant received a certificate. "They had fun." They also learned about something that probably wouldn't have interested them otherwise. A Tourism Writing course could offer the same opportunity.

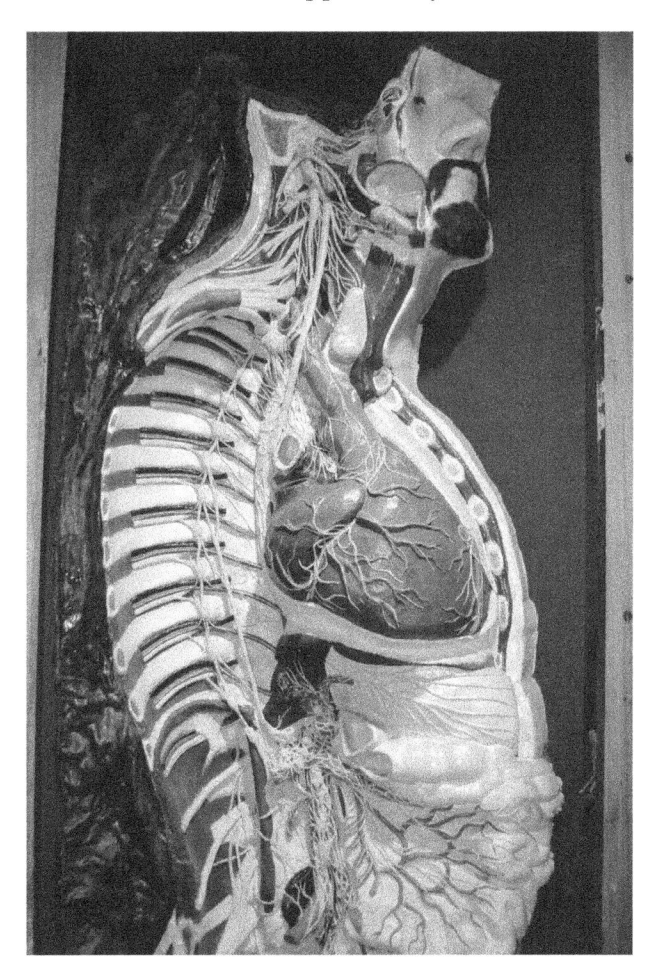

Anatomical Figure.

Passionate about his own work, Glassbrook progressively looks to the future. He feels the key to getting schools involved is to start with teachers of liberal arts and identify certain objectives this project fits with. On a college level, it could also involve business and technical writing courses. If they push the program, Tourism Writing could be the next new course offered to students.

But to convince schools to become involved with this new genre of writing, the word has to be spread. This can be done many different ways. The field of medicine may not seem to be affected, but it is.

A native Mobilian, now living and practicing in Montgomery, Past President Medical Association of State of Alabama; Past President Alabama Academy of Radiology Chapter of American College of Radiology, Dr. David Montiel—the leader of a group of thirty doctors who cover mid-Alabama, Selma, Opelika, and Montgomery serving twenty hospitals—cites one of his problems is to convince radiologists to come to Montgomery. "These doctors have more than one job offer and Montgomery does not have the same panache as coastal cities."

He mentioned that they have to compete with areas with beaches but stressed, "Alabama has a lot of tourist attractions, but the perception by the rest of the country, in general, is that Alabamians are back-woodsy and unsophisticated rednecks. There's almost a subconscious stereotype about the South." He added that is due, in part, to the movie and television portrayal of Southerners as "ignorant old coots."

He saw hope for that attitude to change because at Montgomery's regional hospital for the Air Force at Maxwell Field doctors coming to practice there changed their image. "Tourism writing could have a similar impact by educating people. Besides," he said, "people who move to the Sun Belt learn to like the easy life—and not just the weather."

When asked about how best to market Tourism Writing he suggested tying it in to marketing. "Businesses pay for marketing services and they might hire someone to write about tourism to promote it. Gulf Coast hotels depend on tourism to sell. Tourism Writing is a skill marketers could use."

Another Emergency Room doctor, Philip Levin of Biloxi, MS, also a published author, said, "Tourism pieces sell well. I paid my way through medical school writing tourism articles, and I went to Greece. It excites to see photos of places; it makes them want to visit. Articles about local places are easy to write. I wrote twenty-five articles about places and events on the Mississippi Gulf Coast."

Dr. Levin saw another bonus for Tourism Writing. "Tourism brings in potential medical people who make good recruits as doctors. If they are considering taking up residence in an area, they want to know what there is to see and do. If they like the options, they may stay." He smiled. "Tourism also brings patients, {people} who come to see the area and get sick."

Judge Jim Fraiser, author of *The Majesty of Mobile*, from Pass Christian in Harrison County, a man who has seen much of the seedy side of life in his career, also saw the benefits of Tourism Writing. "Tourism Writing can educate kids about interesting things, like culture. And learning about things they would never have known about otherwise helps them stay away from gangs." His statement is on target. Making youths aware of a sense of worthwhile values by exposing them to art and history can lead them in a different direction. Doing so may result in taking them off the streets and away from gang activity into a cultural world previously unknown to them, a worthy goal. As they say of teachers, "If you can reach just one person..." You can't save everybody. Some people *LIVE*, others are content to simply *EXIST*. Their lifestyle lets them sleep late, then spend the day in pajamas, eating, playing computer games and watching TV—then back to bed. Others *LIVE*, learning something new every day, working, communicating and meeting new people and exploring new places—being productive. Perhaps causing one young person to change his or her lifestyle and become aware of the beauty of life and moving away from a useless life or a life of crime is worth the effort.

17
UNUSUAL INFLUENCES

In trying to attract tourists, writers must consider a variety of options. The expression *Different strokes for different folks* definitely applies. My interest in crime scenes after testifying in a bank robbery trial took me to North Carolina to see the lake where Susan Smith drowned her children, and also to Pelican Point in Alabama where another woman drove her car into the water and her children drowned. I also visited the house in Salem, Massachussets, where the witch trials were held—a crime because innocent people were hung as a result of the judge's rulings.

Some people have a morbid interest in cemeteries, or perhaps they seek history from inscriptions on graves. It surprised me that many entries in the last SELTI contest were about graveyards. However, they did show how such places were interesting enough to draw visitors.

But it's not just the attraction of a place. Although we may originally visit it because it interests us, what we frequently take away and remember are the people we meet in a particular location. For example, a few years ago, I saw Al Hirt perform in New Orleans. About a dozen people were seated at each table. We were packed tight, a chummy situation. My seatmate introduced himself as an owner of a trucking business in the Midwest. The intense enthusiasm and energy of Al Hirt and his pianist kept the crowd involved, but at break time, my seatmate and I chatted. He was enthralled with the south and my stories of Mobile celebrating Mardi Gras with parades before New Orleans. I don't recall his name, but I do remember that two weeks later he wrote a letter.

"Before we met," he said, "most of what I heard about Alabama was negative. Now, I have a different impression. I really enjoyed our conversation and learning about Alabama and Mobile."

It felt good to know I'd served as an ambassador for my state and my city.

Other people look for things related to their occupation. On a trip to Jerusalem our guide took us to a hospital. One room was filled with Marc Chagall paintings. Most of the guests stayed in that room, but one lady, an internist, headed for the emergency room. I suppose she was looking for a busman's holiday. But that wasn't all I recall about the visit to the hospital, something else happened that was amusing. One man didn't make it to the bus on time, so we left without him. I often wondered how he got back to the hotel, probably by taxi.

One of the avenues available is obvious—Welcome Centers. Except for Alaska and Hawaii because of their unique geographical locations, every state has them; many have a dozen or more.

A man who once worked for an airline, Grady Earnheart, is now Assistant Manager of the Florida I-10 Welcome Center. He works hard. Extensive research is done for the entire state to get knowledge to offer visitors, along with their famous orange juice.

Florida vies with North and South Dakota to claim to be the first Welcome Center in existence. Regardless of who has lawful claim to that, Earnheart says Tourism Writing could be helpful to any Welcome Center. "Locals don't realize what we provide here. We give information, but if we encourage visitors to stay longer, they spend more money. If we offer them more options, they'll come back often."

The Welcome Center is not a state agency. It is funded by the legislature. It's independent, not the Department of Transportation or Economic Development. And tourism is Florida's number one industry. They cooperate with Visit Florida to increase tourism. But, as Earnheart pointed out, "It's a lot of work with small single owner business." Maybe Tourism Writing could ease their load.

The importance of a warm welcome became evident to me three times in foreign countries. The first time was on a Danube Cruise.

Because of a taxi driver, I loved Bratislava, Slovakia. What does that have to do with Tourism Writing? A lot. To begin with, visiting that far away country makes visitors aware of the charm of cities in different parts of the world.

Much of the appeal was the attention of the female taxi driver who had a daughter in the U.S. and was very interested in learning about our country. Communicating was easy because she spoke English very well. Off the meter, on her own time, she escorted us around. She led us up a hill to visit a beautiful old church and see a gorgeous view. We saw things most visitors never discover and experienced an ambiance only possible when business turns to friendship.

Another incident was in Rome. I've only had a man kiss my hand twice in my life—once years ago at the Coliseum after chatting with a Brazilian engineer and recently by a 106 year old World War II veteran who was General Patton's quartermaster when I presented him a poem I'd written honoring his service. Both were special, but the vet's show of affection touched me most.

The third time I had such an encounter was on a city bus in Sydney, Australia. On the way to the famous Opera House, I sat opposite two ladies. One asked where I was from and after chatting a few moments, she said, "I'm a Brigidine nun and we're going to a tea at the church." She leaned over and touched my hand. "Would you like to come along?"

I wish I could have gone. She was so friendly I wrote a poem about the incident in the hotel that night entitled, *A Prayer between Us,* It was published, and I wanted to send it to her, but I only had her name, no address. Six months later, I received a note from her. I was surprised because I'd forgotten I'd given her my business card.

She was elated to receive the poem. We corresponded frequently and every month, she'd send me their church bulletin. I always read all of it and learned things about Australia I'd never know otherwise. Some of their ministry was with Amnesty International. Once, she was able to telephone me. I invited her to visit, but she had already taken the one big trip those nuns were allowed. "We'll have to meet again in Heaven," she quipped.

One day about ten years later, my letter to her was returned, marked "Deceased." She's gone, but my memories of her warm welcome and the sharing of life experiences remain. Still, I hope our next meeting is a long way off.

\#

The motto: *Honor the Past; Inspire the Future; Promote Patriotism*, the Charter of the Naval Aviation Museum Foundation, expresses its message in a few words.

Although the museum which opened in 1963 is free to enter, due to so many terrorist activities nowadays, security is more important than ever. However, Historian Hill Goodspeed said, "We still want to be seen hospitable. Tourism Writing can help us show that image by letting people know what we do here and what surrounds you. That makes people feel more welcome.

"Being the home of the Blue Angels is the big attraction," he added. "It's unusual here. The public doesn't know that's not the only thing we offer. We want them to get that message. Our Navy story is a reflection of all in the U.S. who serve from all the country—all types. This Pensacola museum tells the national story. Since the Foundation doesn't do a lot of marketing, we can use something like Tourism Writing to get our message out."

In addition to a multitude of planes from the past, they have the well-stocked Emil Buehler Library, which opened in 1992 with books focusing on the development of U.S. Naval Aviation from 1911 to the present. Adults from all over the U.S. and beyond pack this military and aerospace museum daily, alongside students from K-12 taking walking tours. All learn the history of the past.

The Naval Aviation Museum Foundation also sponsors a Flight Adventure Deck Summer Camp on NAS Pensacola. In one week, fifth and sixth grade students can launch their own rocket, experience things like a Giant Screen movie or flight simulators, build gliders, or see a Blue Angels' practice when they are available.

Goodspeed said when the museum started collecting oddities one of the first aircraft they received to help them tell the story of aviation was an inflatable plane packaged in a small box designed to be dropped to pilots shot down behind enemy lines. "It was an experiment and was never used. But the irony is that it was really an Army plane with ARMY printed on its side and it was donated to our Navy Museum."

Marketing Tourism Writing as courses struck Goodspeed as "a valuable tool." He said, "Such writing in a professional style gives a concise, compelling story which fits well in the age in which we live. People who don't tend to read would find Tourism Writing appealing because it's something not connected to writing about abstract things." He felt people could connect and be interested in reading about real places like the museum and learning about other points of interest nearby enough to respond to the direct invitation to visit. www.nam.com

People who own airplanes have a convenience if they want to visit. In nearby Orange Beach, Alabama the Jack Edwards National Airport is a place they can leave their planes. Former Congressman Jack Edwards was responsible for getting this eight hundred and fifty acre U.S. Navy property transferred to the State of Alabama. Fueling is available and hanger space can be rented by the night, week, or month. From this in-town airport, rental vehicles make it easy to reach nearby attractions such as the beach two miles north, and golf courses or fishing spots. It's an accommodation some pilots might not know about—unless they learn of this facility through Tourism Writing.

Gulf Shores Beach.

Lu Lu's.

Jack Edwards National Airport.

Another group that could benefit from Tourism Writing is bird watchers. When asked about this Dr. John Borom, director of Coastal Alabama Community College, Fairhope, AL and President of Mobile Bay Audubon Society, had much to contribute.

First, he talked about the Birdfest, saying, "The Alabama Coastal BirdFest is a birding and nature festival that features trips and opportunities to see birds, alligators, wildflowers, dolphins, and other wildlife and learn about their habitats. Workshops are offered at 5 Rivers Delta Center on hummingbirds, nature photography, and basics of birding. BirdFest highlights great bird-and-nature-watching spots all around Baldwin and Mobile Counties, including Fort Morgan, Dauphin Island, Weeks Bay, Mobile-Tensaw Delta, Bayou La Batre, Forever Wild Grand Bay Savanna, Gulf Shores, Bon Secour River, Fly Creek, Alligator Alley (a gator rescue facility), and more. BirdFest is a great adventure no matter your level of birding experience. Trips are filled in the order registrations are received. The Bird & Conservation Expo is a free, family friendly event that takes place at the Halstead Amphitheater on the grounds of Coastal Alabama Community College in downtown Fairhope, with exhibits, a raptor show, snake show, kids' activities, and more."

He added, "Of the 447 bird species listed for the entire state of Alabama, 442, or about 95 percent have been observed in Baldwin and Mobile Counties. Many of these can be seen in the proper season and habitat at sites along the 240 mile long Alabama Coastal Birding Trail which ties together the best birding locations in the two counties. One hundred and thirty, or 30 percent, of the 422 listed species breed in Baldwin and Mobile Counties."

BirdFest has brought people from about 40 states, France, Canada and England to see birds in South Alabama. Sometimes family members come from different areas to enjoy seeing birds together. One man and his wife from north Alabama have attended every Alabama Coastal BirdFest for 14 years.

As Director of the Fairhope Campus, Dr. Borom felt Tourism Writing could be beneficial because all proceeds from The Alabama Coastal BirdFest are used to help secure habitat for birds and wildlife on the Alabama Gulf Coast. He said adding Tourism Writing courses to the curriculum could help students. "Students can learn that festivals can be used to stimulate the economy, promote environmental stewardship and environmental education." And students are our future leaders; the more they know, the better qualified they'll be to lead.

The Connie Hudson Senior Center, which opened in 2008, is a big success. Up to 475 citizens aged fifty-five or older take advantage of its services on a daily basis. It may seem a bit unusual, but Program Supervisor Ashley Flowers said they could be helped by Tourism Writing. "Lots of seniors travel here to help family members with kids. They could use the information to see what we have locally." This would apply to what is available in the center and nearby.

She mentioned that the older generation using their services are "doers who want to see and feel things. They come here to get out of their recliners and keep their brains active." She smiled. "It's social, too. A senior center isn't an old folks home. This is an *active* place. These people aren't like the current generation. They aren't tied to their cell phones texting or checking e-mail. For them, hands-on activities are what they're looking for. Tourism Writing could help explain this, spread the word."

As a supervisor of five centers in Mobile, Ashley looks for new ways to entertain seniors. She brought pickleball, a game similar to tennis, to the center. Since they must focus on needs, not extras because there's no funding for extra action, some questioned her decision. However, it turned out to be a huge success. Her insightfulness extended to Tourism Writing. She said she "loved the idea of Tourism Writing. It's unique. My people are on fixed incomes looking to get the most for their money. We do local things that are free like attending concerts, riding the trolley and going to museums. And they love the Duck Boats. Discovering new interesting places that are free or inexpensive would be a big help."

In a sensitive vein, Ashley expressed her understanding that some of these seniors are experiencing grief. "People experiencing grief, for example, men who've lost their wives and are trying to make it on their own without a clue as to what to do, need our help. We become their family." She said, "Some don't have anyone else and they only see their children once a year. So we try to connect them to the world." A new challenge providing a distraction, such as writing, could help these people cope.

But you can't please everyone and she has to deal with complaints. "Some people can't stand to see others having fun," she said. "They protest about people talking too loud at lunch. Others want more handicapped parking, golf carts to transport them from their cars to the entrance and the quilters ask for more space. Some even fuss if we have a singer."

She told the story of a singer named Wayne, who'd been on oxygen two years. He started singing Elvis songs while off of oxygen and managed to sing forty minutes. "It gave him a purpose," Ashley said. "He's off oxygen now and he has a fan club. Women love Elvis impersonators."

Then came the amusing part. "But the first time I spoke to the crowd about Wayne instead of saying, 'We had forty minutes of Wayne singing without oxygen,' I said, 'We had forty inches of Wayne.' It became a joke."

Since all the center's activities are volunteer-based, Ashley understands the need for all "to get along." She has achieved unifying members so well that when she was going to be transferred to another location, they protested so loudly the transfer was cancelled. Perhaps forming a group involved in a new genre of writing would intensify that unity. Tourism Writing could help in that regard, too.

www.cityofmobilechmrscc

18

HOTELS, AND BED AND BREAKFASTS

The tourism slogan, *HEADS ON BEDS*, meaning enticing visitors to spend the night in a place, is important because people on vacations often spend more freely than they do at home. This is especially true when your product is books. Travelers want something to read at night, on the beach, on a cruise, or in the car while driving from one destination to another. I know this true. My books go with me everywhere I go, and I sell them. But it's also true that other products sell. For example, my walls are full of souvenir plates. Other people collect music, or jewelry, or things like little figurines. Some just find bargains they don't have at home. My friends from France once spent hundreds of dollars for clothing in a discount store and I once saw several members of a cruise staff returning to their ship with as many bags as they could carry.

At any rate, spending the night in a place gives tourists more opportunity to make purchases. This boost to the economy is good, but think about how much more Tourism Writing could appeal to people searching for things to do and places to go. If travelers could find a variety of choices, perhaps they'd be persuaded to stay longer and max out their credit cards. More heads on beds, more revenue.

Fifteen-year innkeepers, Bill and Wendy James, have had some interesting experiences and some that were frightening. When Hurricane Ivan threatened, they weren't prepared. All plywood was sold out, so, while CBS crews filmed their historical home, they dragged boards from the attic of their Victorian Bed and Breakfast and placed the corrugated panels on windows and doors as protection from high winds and hurling obstacles. Luckily, this house, a catalog home, weathered the storm and retained its many original features, such as, original fireplaces, bookcases, and old doorknobs. The walls have not been repainted, either. You can also ascend the full staircase to the attic where the James found old Kate Shepard schoolbooks, boxes with Kate's gloves, family items, letters and receipts from 1799 to the late 1800's.

Why could Tourism Writing benefit the Kate Shepard House? Wendy says, "Because we have so much to offer, people can learn about history here in a relaxed atmosphere with friendly neighbors to aid to the enjoyment of their stay." She leaned forward and smiled. "A blogger who saw some of our Civil War papers we retrieved from the attic called us The King Tut Tomb of the Civil War. What our guests bring to the table are their own unique experiences." In any place a tourist visits, it's not just the amenities, it's how they feel about a place that makes them feel welcome. Such feelings endure long past the visit.

Wendy says, "We want our customers to leave feeling as if we're their friends." She pointed to Beaux, her friendly Chow Chow lounging at her feet. "Dogs are like family," she said. "That's why we let our guests bring their dogs."

Interesting coincidences happen when people meet. Wendy said, "Two strangers visiting once found a common thread by discovering both were hydro-engineers. Not too many of those around. Another couple from a small town in Louisiana building a halfway house for homeless children sat across the dining room table from two former heroin addicts who now preach against drug usage. Both couples were trying to adopt at the time. They were successful. They also formed a bond and kept in touch with each other." Being a part of such an event is bound to be heart-warming for the Kate Shepard proprietors.

Wendy feels that Tourism Writing can be beneficial to all who use it, or share it, to help others learn about life and their culture. With her pleasant manner and knowledge of history, Wendy is in a perfect position at The Kate Shepard House to use Tourism Writing to help promote it and to spread good-will. info@kateshepardhouse.com

Kate Shepard House.

19

BICENTENNIAL

When our forefathers founded the City of Mobile in 1702, they probably never realized its potential. It would have been hard to imagine what this burg would turn into two hundred and fifteen years later.

In 2019, the entire State of Alabama will be two hundred years old. Alabama's Bicentennial Celebration will showcase its natural beauty, featuring mountains to the north and beaches to the south, its diverse population, and its rich history. And ALABAMA 200: Alabama's Bicentennial Commemoration has already begun. Under Chairperson Carolyn Feltus' direction, it started with a kick-off celebration in Mobile, Alabama's oldest city, on May 5, 2017. At the event, Governor Kay Ivey repeatedly spoke of Alabamians being innovative and Tourism Writing is certainly an innovative concept. (Available at Alabama200.org.)

History Professor James Day at the University of Montevallo, Chairman of the Alabama Historical Commission and Bicentennial

Historian said, "Tourism Writing can assist local communities and counties in celebrating their districts. It gets them in touch with their social and cultural heritage, who they are and where they live." He mentioned that Fort Toulouse/Fort Jackson in Wetumpka, AL—where Andrew Jackson first met with French settlers and Native Americans and imposed his treaty on the defeated Creeks—is an interesting site. He also said, "By using funds from the Bicentennial Committee, they're giving a village in Huntsville a facelift."

Professor Day said it is unusual to have a three year celebration with the first year, 2017, looking at territorial history, the second year, 2018, as a transition and the third year, 2018, statehood.

All sixty-seven Alabama counties will be included. It will stretch from Tuscumbia to Thomasville and Montgomery and Birmingham to Dothan. It will include a diversity of culture and history of people beginning in 2017 with *Discovering Our Places.* In 2018, the theme will be *Honoring Our People*. In 2019, *Sharing Our Stories* will mark the conclusion.

This far-reaching event is a great opportunity to remember our past history, honor those who broke ground in the state, learn from their experiences, and to look to the future for all possibilities to make Alabama even greater.

What better way to elaborate on the aforementioned themes than with Tourism Writing?

20
ENTERTAINMENT

Scott Tindle, co-owner of the Fort of Colonial Mobile, a building they lease from the City of Mobile, said their goal is "to change the branding." They celebrate the different countries that ruled Mobile since it was founded in 1702. For example, they celebrate the American rule with its flag of fifteen stars in July. In June, they celebrated Spanish Rule.

Gulf Coast Ducks started operation in June, 2016 as a private enterprise with three boats and a thirty-five person capacity. On wheels they travel on land and then they move into the water as boats. When they are busy, all three boats are used at the same time.

From the fort and from the *Battleship Alabama*, Duck Boats carrying visitors tie downtown Mobile to different bodies of water. On these seventy-minute guided tours, the Duck Boats go into Mobile River, through downtown Mobile, and into Mobile Bay, all to the thrill of their passengers. "We are trading people's time for fun," Tindle explained. "We have a captive audience learning about the

Battleship USS Alabama and the Duck Boat.

Fort of Colonial Mobile.

ENTERTAINMENT › 137

history of the area. Walt Disney coined the term 'Edutainment' in the fifties—meaning education and entertainment are combined." The goal is to enhance tourism. Tindle said, "We want to show the history of Mobile under French, British, Spanish, Confederate, and American flags and to sell the future, to show what this city can become."

Tindle has seen some unusual and often amusing things. One day he was at the Battleship and saw a man standing by his RV crying. "I stopped to ask if I could help," Scott said.

The man pointed to the top of his car. "Someone stole my air conditioner. It's gone."

"I looked at the vacant space and asked, 'Did you just come from downtown Mobile'? The man nodded. 'Yeah, I came through the Bankhead Tunnel.'"

Scott smiled. "I kept a straight face when I told him I knew what happened to his air conditioner—the clearance in that tunnel is thirteen feet and his a/c raised up to sixteen feet."

Maybe if that man had read about the Bankhead Tunnel and the Wallace Tunnel via Tourism Writing, he'd have taken the route across Cochran Bridge and he'd still have an air conditioner on top of his RV.

The Duck Boat ride was a true adventure. Captain Chris piloted the boat built in 1942 (now rebuilt) while tour guide Adam told the history of the area. Our first dip took us past the Renaissance Hotel and the RSA Tower and we learned about the Moon Pie Drop at midnight on New Year's Eve. When we reached downtown Mobile on land, he mentioned that Water Street was once paved with bricks from Fort Conde when it was torn down. Later, the fort was rebuilt.

Proving Mobilians appreciate culture, he pointed out one of twelve giant painted oysters now decorating the streets of the city.

He also mentioned that there's a bee farm on top of the Admiral Hotel and the two hotel restaurants use the honey from those bees.

As we passed Barton Academy, built in 1835 and used as a school but vacant since 2005, he said it will soon be used as a magnet school.

Next, came the Mobile Public Library, which was voted in the top fifty most beautiful libraries in the U.S. by Town and Country Magazine in 2017. In the entertainment district on Dauphin Street, he noted that the former Convent of Mercy has plaques relating the history of the Sisters of Mercy. Now the buildings are the St. Francis Place Condominiums.

Testifying to our appreciation of good food, he pointed to Wintzell's Oyster Bar, a popular restaurant, saying, "It has now expanded as far as Pennsylvania.

Another attraction is the street art. Painters are allowed to draw on abandoned buildings as long as their work is not offensive and is uplifting and we saw beautiful examples of what some call graffiti."

Adam told about a secret tunnel from long ago which connected the Basilica of the Immaculate Conception to a speak-easy across the street where one could go through the cathedral to the bar. He also said there used to be a cemetery in what is now the popular Cathedral Square but it overflowed and bodies were exhumed and moved to Church Street Cemetery.

When we reached the famous Bienville Square, he mentioned that Bienville, who often wore only a loincloth, had serpent tattoos from his neck down. He felt it helped him get along with traders.

Passing the Battle House Hotel, he said it is famous for two things—its Crystal Ballroom, a scene of many weddings, and its whispering arch. The arch, which allows people to hear whispers from fifty feet across the room, is one of sixty in the world. Proposals have been made across that room and on Halloween, a joker often stands in one corner and tries to frighten an unsuspecting listener in the other.

Back in the water, for the triple splash, Scott said, "The Delta is known as the Amazon of America." He added while passing Cooper Park, "It's the only waterfront park around open to the public. The portal, the Port of Alabama, can get you anywhere in the world you want to go."

An oddity is that the DUKW (duck boats) were built by women. The amphibious crafts were known by factory serial letters: D stands for Date, 1942, year of origin; U stands for Utility, land to water; K stands for Car, all wheel drive; and W stands for Dual Tandem Rear Axle. "No W there." Adam grinned. "I think it really stands for women." Another source says the W stands for six wheels.

We also passed Austal, which employs 4,200 people. It had a full parking lot, along with a rack of bicycles provided for those who don't want to walk a mile from their parking spot to the building's entrance.

On returning to Battleship Park, we drove by sixty-seven oaks in the shape of Alabama, representing Alabama's sixty-seven counties. It also has blue sidewalks representing the state's rivers.

We saw planes, not damaged by war but by Hurricane Katrina when they were washed out of their hanger. It's nice to know volunteers are in the process of repairing them and preserving history. But you have to *know* history to understand its importance. Tourism Writing can help inform people of the need to preserve it and inspire them to take action.

So can good will. During the busy 2017 Labor Day weekend, Scott Tindle sent all three of his Duck Boats on a mission of mercy.

They went to Houston, Texas, in the wake of Hurricane Harvey, to transport dialysis patients to places for treatment. One man had gone a week without dialysis. It probably saved his life, along with saving the lives of others dependent on treatment to survive. At great loss of revenue for their owner, Mobile Ducks served a dual purpose. Along with physical help maybe only they could provide, their services proved Mobilians' compassion—not just in words, but also in deeds.

Mobile has much more to offer. For football, we have two bowl games, the Senior Bowl, an All-Star game, and the Go-Daddy Bowl, plus the University of South Alabama's Jaguar games. Other local colleges and high schools have baseball, basketball, volleyball, football, and soccer, and the Bay Bears play baseball at Hank Aaron Stadium. www.laddpeeblesstadium.org

Both Bellingrath and the Botanical Gardens provide colorful flowers and Bellingrath puts on quite a show at Christmas. Three community theaters—the Joe Jefferson Playhouse, the Mobile Theater Guild and the Chickasaw Civic Theater—all provide live shows for their audiences, as does Playhouse in the Park.

The Joe Jefferson Playhouse is the oldest continuously operating theater in Alabama. In seventy years of producing plays many things have changed. Its older patron base presents a challenge. Many have died. Longtime volunteer and actor, Jason McKenzie, who recently became JJP's executive director, has the goal of "keeping it alive." To do so, it is necessary to appeal to a new group of younger people and McKenzie wants to "be in the forefront of that." It is a necessary consideration in the wake of a decline in subscriptions for the season.

Over the years ticket prices haven't changed much. However, in the past, patrons had to buy season tickets for all fie productions.

Now those tickets can be used five times for one show or once each for a show. Also, tickets are available for one show. "You can build your own program," McKenzie said, noting that with modern technology, "we are a fast moving society of last minute people." So such a versatile option is warranted.

Preserving JJP is worth the effort. It is unique because it's uncommon for a theater to be located in a neighborhood. Residents and Murphy High School surround the area. It's accessible and they have minimal overhead. They don't pay actors or a staff; most are volunteers. Since Mobile is below sea level, they found a way to save money by having a moat in their prop room. When the building floods, McKenzie said, "We sweep water into the moat and a sump sucks the water out fine."

However, they had unexpected expense when a tornado hit Mobile in 2012 and closed them down for months. "It took off most of the roof. We lost our historic lamppost. The city replaced that with an exact model," McKenzie bragged. But they never found their sign; replacing that is on his list. In the seventeen years, he's been involved with the theater, he has found the dedication of the volunteers impressive saying, "JJP is in their blood."

He has high ambitions. "My biggest goal is to sell out every show. Not for financial reasons; I want people to enjoy the plays and the actors earn the right to be seen." McKenzie takes the responsibility for making it work. "It's our job to make it happen. It's a good way to see how the theater puts Mobile flavor into any performance."

Will the ghost some say inhabits the premises help, or will it take something like Tourism Writing to keep JJP alive another seventy years? Who-oo knows?

Joe Jefferson Playhouse.

www.joejeffersonplayers.com
www.mobiletheaterguild.org
cctshows.com
www.playhouseinthepark.org

Mobile's downtown Art Walk increases its traffic annually leading walkers past the quaint Crescent Theater. The new OWA amusement park at The Wharf will attract more visitors to Orange Beach and the surrounding area. Plus, Carnival Cruise Lines in now back in Mobile at their terminal near the GulfQuest National Maritime Museum of the Gulf Coast.

Led by Executive Director Brent Beall, with a staff of twelve, the GulfQuest Museum includes over ninety exhibits including theaters, stimulators and displays. Some exhibits are interactive. Their mission statement is "To inspire people of all ages and backgrounds to understand and appreciate the Gulf Coast's rich maritime heritage through exhibits, programs and activities." www.gulfquest.org

The renovated Gulf, Mobile, & Ohio Railroad Building, a historic landmark, is a Spanish Mission Revival architectural site worth viewing. Located at the head of Water Street in downtown Mobile's central business district, it is the most recognizable building in south Alabama. It was completed in 1907 and was a passenger railroad terminal until the late 1950's, then served as an office building. It had an eighteen million-dollar renovation in 2003. Owned by the City of Mobile, the GM&O building offers leasehold interest—a chance to invest in a landmark that's historic. http://www.peeblesandcameron.com/listings_detail.php?listing=253

As always, fishing, a sport that's extremely popular, is available at no cost, except for the license required. It's considered to be the best money making sport in the U.S. According to the University of South Alabama's Dr. Bob Shipp, head of the Marine Sciences Department, between 15,000 and 20,000 artificial reefs in the Gulf provide fish habitats (*Great Days Outdoors Magazine*, March 2013, page 46).

And Craig Newton, a biologist with Alabama Marine Resources says, "While recreational fishing in Alabama creates a $797 million revenue stream, 90 percent of offshore trips are associated with

Alabama's 15,000 offshore reefs. This is despite the fact that our coast makes up only five percent of the Gulf of Mexico coastline (*Great Days Outdoors Magazine*, February 2014, page 9).

Newton is also Alabama's artificial reef coordinator. Alabama already has the largest artificial reef in the country and is about to add another 250-foot surveying boat to it. He said in addition to money spent in that area, the state benefits from tourists' taxes at hotels and restaurants when people visit the reef to fish.

Tom Steber reinforced his opinion saying Alabama was the pioneer of the reef system and without it, we would have no bottom fish. It began with putting out car bodies and evolved into getting federal funding, using tanks and liberty ships (*Great Days Outdoors Magazine*, February 2014, page 9).

In 2014, a network of cement statues provided the perfect depth for novice and youth divers—Poseidon's Playground. Lila Harris, dive instructor and underwater photographer, was a driving force for the project. More is planned. Newton and other state officials are working on a grant proposal including more BP money from the Naitonal Fish and Wildlife Foundation (Mullen, John, Contributing Editor, *Lagniappe Weekly* 8-3-17—8-9-17).

The Alabama Deep Sea Fishing Rodeo, an annual event on Dauphin Island held in July, draws over 3,000 participants. The three-day event began in 1939, a Jaycees project, it includes youth as well as adults and offers a chance for many anglers to prove their skills and win valuable prizes for their expertise. The $200,000 the ADSFR has donated to the University of South Alabama Department of Marine Sciences helps fund academic scholarships (http://adsfr.com/about_rodeo.html).

A stress relieving sport, fishing provides significant health benefits. Such physical activity helps lower public health care costs by reducing obesity rates. It has additional benefits, as does other outdoor recreation. Executive Director of the hunting Heritage Foundation Corky Pugh cites a report by the Outdoor Industry Association Southwick Associates which states, "...investments in outdoor recreation could significantly reduce crime rates, improve educational outcomes for many children..."

A few lucky people may experience seeing a Mobile Bay Jubilee. This anomaly is thought to happen only in this area and in Tokyo Bay, Japan. These unpredictable events occur in the summertime on a fifteen-mile stretch from Fairhope to Mullet Point, usually just before sunrise. Conditions have to be just right—cloudy, a calm bay and a rising tide. When fish, crabs, flounder and eels lack oxygen, they can't swim and end up on shore. As soon as someone discovers a Jubilee has occurred, the cry "Jubilee! Jubilee!" causes people to flock to the scene with nets and containers, scooping up all they can carry away. Unfortunately, you can't plan a visit to coincide with a Jubilee because no one can tell when one will happen.

These are far from all attractions. Tourism Writing can clue you in as to what else is available, but you have to decide what you want to see and do.

21
HOMELESS

If you think the homeless aren't involved in tourism, think again. They can be an influence, even if in an unusual way. An odd happening proves this point.

A few weeks ago, I rode to Wells Fargo bank with a friend. When Liz drove up to the service window and the teller slid out the drawer, I handed Liz my deposit slip folded over a check. It was an extremely windy day and just as she put the deposit in the tray, the wind whipped up and blew it away. I watched it fly over the hood of the car and tumble forward. Then, like a kite lifted by a gust of wind, it soared and disappeared. What goes up must come down, but I was unable to determine where it landed.

The bank manager witnessed what happened and came out to help. For twenty minutes, she, Liz, and I looked up and down the street in all directions. No luck. It was nowhere to be found. I regretted losing the money but I'm glad it was only one check for less than fifty dollars.

As we gave up our search and returned to the car, a woman in out of style clothes approached holding a tiny black kitten. It couldn't have been more than two weeks old. "It was wandering around Checkers next door. I couldn't let it get run over by a car and killed," she told us. "I'm new here and I'm homeless; I can't keep it." Her eyes became misty as she reached in her bag, pulled out a half eaten hamburger, and held it up. "I can't feed that cat; I can barely feed myself. I got this out of the dumpster. It's all I have to eat today. So, I took a couple of bites and I'm saving the rest for supper." She held out the kitten. "Can one of you take it?"

My compassionate friend took the furry little creature, which fit into the palm of one hand. "I'll take care of it, until I can find her a permanent home." Liz pulled a twenty-dollar bill out of her purse and handed it to the woman.

Stuffing the money in her pocket and muttering, "Thank you," the woman scurried away.

Liz moistened her lips. "I feel sorry for her, but she ran off before I could offer to do anything else. I guess there's nothing more we can do for her anyway."

We drove away with the cat snuggled against my friend's shoulder. "You told me you're allergic to cats," I said. "How are you going to handle that helpless little kitten?"

"Oh, I'll take her to the vet, and I'll get a prescription for antihistamines for myself and hope they work. There goes another twenty a week co-pay. Woe is me." She gave me a sideways glance. "But I had to save that poor little baby. She'd get killed out on the highway in five minutes. Besides, I had to show we cared. I couldn't let that woman get the wrong impression of our city."

The woman is most likely still homeless. The cat now lives like a raj and has her way with her new owner. I was wrong; that little beast sure isn't helpless. It has destroyed plants, messed up the entire house, and scratched and bitten Liz. She named her unmanageable new pet for me and the bank—Mary Wells, but she calls it, "The devil cat from Hell."

Mary Wells is picky. She eats only expensive Fancy Feast Medleys food at two-fifty a day. Because of lactose intolerance, she has to have Whiskers Cat Milk that costs a dollar and a half a pop, and she'll only drink it if it's heated. She's choosy about the litter in her box, too. If it isn't the Breeze brand, which requires disposable pads running the cost up to twenty dollars a week, she won't use it. More mess elsewhere. That darn cat is spoiled.

She's high-maintenance in every way. In addition to normal vet bills, when Liz gets fed up, she boards her at the vet a few days. They say, "When she's here, she's well behaved and sweet as sugar." They fawn over her. They don't enjoy her enough to care for her for free, though, and their fees add to the price of her upbringing. Kitty cat is costing as much as raising a child. At home, she continues to misbehave, slipping into rooms where she doesn't belong, dragging anything she can move under the bed, and even trying to escape outside. She also loves water. When confined to the bathroom, her private domain, she jumps into the washbowl and manages to turn on the faucet, and then she splashes water everywhere.

"She's more than a catastrophe, she's a cat-astrophel—you know, a bitter herb," Liz said. "I was so desperate after dealing with her one day, I asked the vet, 'How much is an exorcist and do you know one?'" Like most cats, Miss Independent goes where she wants and does as she pleases. I guess it's true that we can own a dog, but a cat owns us.

Liz has already spent over a thousand dollars on that animal and is shelling out more daily. At least that money and the twenty dollars the homeless woman has no doubt spent fed the economy. Maybe, in an uncommon way, it will pay off more. I have an idea. If it works, it could turn a negative into a positive, at least in part. I think I can convince my reporter friend that Liz's rescuing an abandoned kitten is a newsworthy act of kindness and she'll do a story on it. However, the real story may be the irony that the cat got a home but the woman didn't. Either one is good PR. Plus, if people read about the devil cat here, perhaps this Tourism Writing will show the good will and compassion of Mobilians and entice folks to visit.

Mary Wells

22
FARMING

We don't always think about it, but bees are vital to the existence of humans. A big proportion of the food we eat is provided by them, in one way or another.

Bees play their part in pollinating vegetables and fruits that humans eat. They also pollinate food for animals that supply us with meat. Foraging crops, such as field beans and clover, are vital to those animals' survival.

Two other products from the bees' courtesy are honey and wax. Honeybees contribute significantly to our wellbeing.

A colony of 50,000 bees can pollinate 4,000 fruit trees and make an average of 14kg of honey. One-third of food is pollination dependent and all bees pollinate 70 types of crops and make 6,000 tons of honey contributing 400,000 Pounds (521,934.29 dollars) to the economy (http://www.bbc.co.uk/guides/zg4dwmn#zc3c4wx).

These tiny creatures, which may only be about 15mm long, have special adaptations to maximize pollen and nectar from flowers.

But now honeybees are in trouble (Packham, Chris, naturalist and presenter).

Honeybees are independent. They have the ability to defend themselves against attack and they can fly for miles searching for food, plus being able to survive harsh winters. However, they need certain basic things to survive and are subject to multiple problems. They must have water to cool the hive and dissolve crystallized honey. They also need quiet; loud noises disturb them. They must have a source of nectar and pollen in the summer, along with warm weather. Their body temperatures must be above 57F in the winter, which requires shelter and stored honey so they can stay inside and be warm for months.

An overzealous beekeeper, too much heat or cold, or a dead queen can all create problems. Their main problems in any part of the world are: disease, pests, pesticides and Colony Collapse Disorder.

Disease is a huge problem in beekeeping and some diseases are suspected of causing Colony Collapse. Honeybees have enemies in nature. Bears do love honey. Mites and mice are threats, too. Humans add to the problem by using pesticides and those chemicals aren't choosey about what they kill. The compromise is for beekeepers to ask neighbors to let them know when they'll spray pesticides and move the bees three miles away from the area for a day.

(http://www.perfectbee.com/a-healthy-beehive/main-threats-to-bees)

Saving the bees is important and awareness is the key.

While bees are vital to humans, so is farming, not just raising vegetables and fruit but also raising cattle, including dairy farming. Some of this has lost favor. Arnie Cink, whose family's dairy farm dates back to the 1950's, stressed its importance.

"In the 1950's, Baldwin County (AL) had 150 dairies and two dairy processing plants—Graham and Woodhaven Dairy. Now there are almost none in Baldwin County."

The exceptions are Borden's Dairy in Robertsdale, a branch business now categorized under Condensed Evaporated Milk and Sweet Home Farm tucked away in a corner of Elberta. The former site of Woodhaven Dairy in Silverhill, AL is often visited by tourists who've heard stories of its being haunted by two young children who drowned in a well there.

Sweet Home is a small, quaint shop with a variety of cheeses. It is a working family dairy established in Baldwin County, Alabama in 1985. It was the first licensed farmstead cheese maker in Alabama. The cheese produced on their farm is made solely from their own herd's milk.

Friendly owners of this small operation, Alyce Birchenough and Doug Wolbert, are committed to handcrafting a wide variety of raw milk cheeses to offer customers. All their cheese is aged for 60 days and made from fresh cows milk, culture, salt and enzymes. The upscale Dauphin's Restaurant in downtown Mobile offers a cheese plate with selections from Sweet Home.

Store location:
27107 Schoen Road, Elberta Alabama 36530
Open: Weekend hours
Telephone: (251) 986-5663
www.onlyinourstate.com/alabama/cheese-farm-al/

But Cink feels young people may not know about such places or even dairy farms in general. "You can ask kids where milk comes from and they don't know. Some may say chocolate milk comes from brown cows." He stressed the importance of preserving history, saying he belongs to an Antique Tractor Club. "We shell and grind corn, dig potatoes and team horses—just for fun. It's important to know your heritage. Everyone needs to know where they're coming from. The new generation should know what their grandparents did. Years ago, more people made their livelihood farming." He indicated that, with changes, it could work again, saying, "Anytime you look back on history, if things don't work, you shouldn't do them again. Find a new way." With all the labor saving modern equipment and machinery, including creature comforts like air-conditioned tractors, it shouldn't be too difficult. In fact, farming should be easier, and perhaps more lucrative, than ever before, despite stringent government regulations.

If people can be persuaded to improve their working conditions, contribute to the common good, and preserve their heritage by learning about it through Tourism Writing, it's a benefit worth consideration.

23

NASHVILLE

Brian Jones, media-specialist for the Alabama Tourism Department agrees with other experts, saying, "Tourism Writing brings attention to the state and promotes travel to our events and attractions." However, this is not limited to Alabama. It extends to all states and cities. It is especially true regarding Music City, Nashville, Tennessee.

Even though some people say there's no such thing as coincidence, others feel everything that happens is destined, part of a plan. Yesterday, my feeling that coincidences do occur was tested. In Nashville, TN, I met Bill Sparkman who spends time between Nashville and Mobile because he owns property in both places. In our conversation, he mentioned the importance of preserving history, saying, "I've been researching one piece of my property on Broad Street. It was once the Mobile Leather Company."

What? My eyes widened. My next-door neighbor's family once owned a leather company.

Bill said he'd researched at the Mobile Public Library but didn't find much information. "They probably rented the building. I didn't find any photos. Things get away and then they're gone and so is history. You can't get it back."

He's right; once historical photos and records are lost, they can't be retrieved.

As it turned out, the Mobile Leather Company wasn't the same company my neighbors owned. But maybe someone will come up with information, records, or photos. So whether our meeting was coincidence or fate, hopefully, it will result in the preservation of a bygone commercial business—and the Mobile Leather Company will come to life for future generations.

A bookstore tucked into a section of The Idea Hatchery in Nashville features only local authors. Its genial proprietor, Chuck Beard, said East Side Story has been operating five years. An author himself, Chuck wrote *Adventures Inside A Bright-Eyed Sky*, a touching story of a sensitive young boy's friendships, especially one with an older woman who gives him good advice even after her death. Chuck calls it, "A modern Huck Finn." Some of his ideas probably came from his work with troubled teens.

According to their flyer, this shop is "a blank canvas for all local literary ideas to help make Music City more of a book town."

Chuck was enthusiastic about Tourism Writing. "It could benefit the community by getting notice and crossing paths with tourists who learn about us. It lets people find things." He said they have unusual requests. One customer pointed to a painting entitled, *Be the person your dog thinks you are* and wanted to commission him to paint a cat and entitle it *Be the person...* She said the painting itself told the story. "Your cat's always looking, judging you."

East Side has more to offer. Twice a month, Korby Lenker does storytelling at East Side Story. But Chuck says his favorite thing that happened was when his son was four months old and his wife returned to work, he kept his son in the shop with him. He felt it was a great experience to have customers be a part of his son's life until the boy went to day care at age sixteen months. Perhaps that will lead to the son following in his father's footsteps someday.

www.EastSideStoryTN.com

Meg MacFadyen, of Art & Invention Gallery, in Nashville, TN, was in her art-stained overalls busily preparing for the upcoming Tomato Art Fest (August 9–12) when we spoke. The schedule of events features everything from a Preview Party of tasty tomato treats to people dressed as fruits and vegetables. It also includes a Children's Fun Run as a fund raiser and a parade with floats pushed, pulled, carried, or worn, and lots of music, art and culture.

Meg felt that Tourism Writing could benefit her business and community by "making people curious about what's happening and they'll want to come to Nashville and to my gallery to see the real thing." She gave an example of why she felt that would work. "The show *Northern Exposure* caused people to look for a fictitious town in Alaska; Tourism Writing would draw people here."

She had a goal when opening her business in 2001. "This neighborhood was diversified," she said, "we had prostitutes to billionaires. All levels of the socio/economic ranks. My intent was to have many styles of art and price points. I wanted to make all feel welcome, so people might find something for themselves that they could afford. One day shortly before Christmas, a lady came in and took a long time looking around. She didn't buy anything but we talked as I showed her different things."

Meg wiped a tear from her eye. "The next day she came back and told me, 'I have no money and I didn't have a thing for my kids for Christmas, not even a tree. But after you showed me around, I got some ideas. I went home and made a tree with what I had.'"

Sometimes goals are fulfilled.

American Pickers Shop.

www.artandinvention.com

Although they were busy preparing for the Fest, Meg talked with some artists who came into the store. One person who does metal art came from Indiana to market his wares. Jason Wright had metal tomatoes and hearts, large and small. He also has had contact with Antique Archaeology in Nashville of the well-known American Pickers TV show.

American Pickers Shop.

Jason's Funky Metal Art.

Jason's Funky Metal Art.

24
CONGRESSIONAL RECORD

Congressman Bradley Byrne recognized the value of Tourism Writing and spoke about it on the Floor of Congress. Entitled, *Highlighting the Value of Tourism through Literature*, it is part of the permanent record which can be found in the Congressional Record, PROCEEDINGS AND DEBATES OF THE 113TH CONGRESS, SECOND SESSION. It reads:

Mr. Speaker, I rise today to honor two outstanding English professors for their innovative contributions toward promoting tourism through literature.

First, Professor Mary S. Palmer's short story "Raisin' Cain" recently won the Southeastern Literary Tourism Initiative Tourism Writing Contest Award.

Professor Palmer's story highlighted the family-friendly nature of Mobile's Mardi Gras and was published online at the Southeastern Literary Tourism Initiative's website. The story includes photos and tourism links at the end so readers can learn how to visit the real Mardi Gras parades and other nearby Mobile attractions included in the inspiring story.

I also want to recognize Dr. Sue Walker who currently teaches tourism writing to several of the English classes at the University of South Alabama in Mobile, Alabama.

Dr. Walker is using the examples of tourism writing from this initiative to challenge her students to compose original short works of literature that encourage their readers to visit the actual places included in the stories.

Mr. Speaker, on Alabama's Gulf Coast, we know just how important tourism is to our local economies. I proudly support any effort to encourage tourism in our region, and I especially applaud innovative methods in the classroom, like tourism writing. Professor Palmer and Dr. Walker have found a unique way to highlight the heritage and culture of South Alabama while providing an enriching experience for their students.

Presentation of Selti Award. October 2014. Names (left to right): Archbishop Thomas Rodi, Guest, Mary S. Palmer, Margaret Daniels, City Councilman Fred Richardson, Congressman Bradley Byrne.

I hope my colleagues in the house will invite their state's writers and teachers to take a look at what is going on in Mobile and consider ways to incorporate these types of college courses into their curriculum, and in turn, highlight their state's unique tourism attractions."

I will be honored to present Professor Palmer with the 2014 SELTI Tourism Fiction Award on October 15 at the Mobile Carnival Museum, and I am excited to highlight these types of innovative teaching methods.

Congressman Bradley Byrne, Patrick Miller.

Opportunities for promotion of this new genre exist. Tourism Writing covers a broad spectrum. It teaches us about other people's cultures such as the history of the Poarch Indians and Kudzu Lewis, who arrived in Plateau on the last slave ship to come to Mobile. It helps us appreciate our diversity and our similarities.

That reminds me of an old nursery rhyme dating back to 1475 in England, which refers to diverse types of occupations. Entitled *Tinker, Tailor*, this counting song begins:

Tinker, tailor, soldier, sailor,
Rich man, poor man, beggar man, thief,
Doctor, lawyer, Indian chief.

While "beggar man" might now be called homeless, and "merchant" is sometimes substituted for "Indian chief", the other occupations remain much the same. However, modern society has added many new occupations to the mix—rocket scientists, astronauts, and computer programmers, along with numerous others.

People who benefit from Tourism Writing fall into these categories, so their input as to how it can benefit them was worth investigating. In these pages, I sought answers to that question by interviewing a homeless woman, heads of corporations and civic organizations, college professors, military personnel, doctors, lawyers, and many others in various occupations. Their responses differed greatly, but none denied Tourism Writing could enhance their lives in some way.

Isn't that reason enough to warrant following Congressman Byrne's suggestion and promoting it as a new genre of writing?

#

The world is smaller now and travel is more accessible than in the past. In traveling to all fifty states, I learned that the more people are different, the more they are the same. We share interests such as sports, amusement parks, gambling casinos, historical spots, and art. Nature's beauty can also be appreciated by all at no cost. Fishing, on top of the list of sporting activities, is also free.

But wherever they go, people respond to a warm welcome. For example, the friendly smiles and spontaneous greetings Mobilians offer visitors makes them agree with the old expression, "Once you have Mobile dirt on your shoes, you want to come back."

This can be true of any city, just as it is with folks who claim Southern Hospitality. Although examples in this book are in Alabama and surrounding states, what happens in Alabama, happens elsewhere. These types of places and events exist in other states. Showing hospitality is up to the residents.

25

WRITE RIGHT AND SHARE ATTRACTIONS TO ENCOURAGE TOURISTS

In discovering all the different perspectives in tourism and the creative art of writing about it, there almost seems to be a need for a textbook. To meet this need, Paula Webb, Patrick Miller and I plan to create a specific textbook for Tourism Writing. Here is an example of how the course can be instructed:

Writing can be a chore, or it can be fun. Tourism Writing can easily fit in the second category. No matter where you live, in the city or the country, chances are you've discovered some place or event many people do not know about but would enjoy seeing. Making strangers aware of those places or events is what Tourism Writing is all about.

Patrick Miller, founder of SELTI, explains the organization's beginning, discusses people influenced by it in different occupations, its far-reaching implications, and ways it can be used in a classroom:

"Tourism Writing began with the Southeastern Literary Tourism Initiative (SELTI) through competitive short story challenges designed to harness the unique creative flexibility of fiction to highlight real locations and attractions around Alabama. The winners of every contest were featured in the media, recognized by local politicians, and published online at the SELTI website. Each online feature included photos of the real attractions highlighted in the story, informational links for readers to learn and explore more, and most importantly a direct invitation for readers to visit.

Although Tourism Writing began with the SELTI project, it has the potential to go far beyond the contests conducted so far. Tourism Writing can go as far as you take it. Introducing the concept is simple enough: write a story set in a real place that readers would be interested in visiting, then invite them to go there and show them how.

How is fiction more "flexible" than nonfiction in promoting tourism? Consider the Kate Shepherd bed and breakfast mentioned earlier in this book. There was a wonderful description of the place, and the photos are beautiful. However, what would appeal to a potential reading tourist more: an informative article about the house (the kind of article that is found in hundreds of bed and breakfast magazines, blogs, and websites)—or a short story that brought the house and its family from 1897 to life in a dramatic scene when the secret Confederate documents were first hidden in the attic? A nonfiction article can speculate on how the documents got there, but a short story can allow readers to witness firsthand what was said and happened in real time as if they were in the attic themselves and participating in the whispers and warnings.

A nonfiction article can describe when a marriage proposal occurred at a certain romantic location, such as Bellingrath Gardens, but a short story can allow readers to feel the heartbeat of a woman about to take a leap of faith on a promise that will change her life forever. A short story will allow readers to experience the waves of excitement with the young man as he builds up the courage to ask the fateful question that will change his life forever. They won't just read about what happened, they will be there, they will see the sun light up her beautiful blue eyes just as he gets down on one knee. They will feel her quickened pulse as he takes her hand in his. You get the idea. There is a difference between what nonfiction can describe and where fiction can *take* the reader.

Most fictional stories, no matter how romantic or mysterious, never ask the reader to step inside the story at the end. However, what reader wouldn't love to do just that? And wouldn't he, or she, want to take someone else along for the trip?

So how does all this happen? Everything starts with you. If you are a writer, set your next story in a place that inspires you, a place that you know readers would love to visit if only someone invited them. When you get ready to submit the query letter for the project to the next literary agent or publisher, mention that the tourism aspect of the work can be promoted in the local and state media as a added draw, publicity that most non-tourism fiction never enjoys. The story itself has to be good on its own, but the extra publicity potentially available will interest the agent or publisher. Show how the tourism element will generate more commissions for them through higher than normal sales. They are competing for market share just like writers, and an extra publicity edge will be very welcome.

Speaking of literary agents, if you happen to be one of those, consider asking for tourism manuscripts, both from prospective clients and current ones. The request may take a year for writers to complete, especially for tourism novels, but if you ask for them, they will come! And when they do, do what you always do: pick the very best and send out polite standardized rejection letters to the hundreds and then thousands of others that come in with them. (Writers, keep in mind that you will be competing with many other tourism writers, so don't expect an easy sell just because the story is tourism related!) Agents, once you have a quality tourism manuscript in hand, get the contract and sell the project to publishers as a publicity-heavy novel or short story collection that will drive up sales like never before. When you sell the book to a publisher, contact the state and city tourism agencies and ask them to help you blitz the media about the tourism dollars that this new book will generate. They are as interested in tourism dollars as you are in commissions and writers are in royalties.

If you are a publisher, put out word to your literary agents that you are looking for tourism manuscripts and anthologies. Literary agents will focus on what you ask for, and they will sort through the low quality submissions to find the rare gems. Often your marketing skills can play the pivotal role in a book's success or failure, but this will help tip the balance towards success with the extra weight of positive publicity. And don't stop with articles and features about the book itself; organize group tours with your readers where they get to visit the places in the novels with hundreds of other people who also loved the books. Tours like that will help build relationships between readers on a whole new level, and that will build loyalty to your publishing house. Group tours will generate higher word-of-mouth than normal novels, and will also fill up hotels faster.

If you are a teacher or educational administrator, especially in creative writing, actively set up courses related to tourism writing. Don't let another university get the credit for developing the nation's top tourism writing program before yours did. Teachers can design courses and degree programs, and administrators can obtain the outside funding necessary to finance them. State legislators who decide higher education funding will be much more inclined to fund a creative writing program that promises to generate tourism dollars than one that just focuses on artistic skills. Most universities have literary magazines, so devote a portion of those to tourism writing projects so students have a platform to practice and hone their work. Larger universities also have academic presses that can publish more professional tourism novels and anthologies that support state attractions to the national market. Finally, as with any academic discipline, regional and national conferences can hone professor's teaching skills by learning from each other. Consider organizing a tourism writing conference and invite the faculty from other universities to attend. Also invite city and state tourism officials as speakers, along with the politicians who might vote on funding future or current tourism writing programs.

If you are a politician, whether a mayor of a small town or president of the United States, start by inviting the writers in your area to focus on tourism attractions. Encourage teaching institutions, even at the high school level, to challenge students to become the next generation of tourism writers by learning the basic skills in the classroom. Encourage literary organizations to seek funding for creative tourism writing projects. Many such organizations already receive funding for writing projects, so why not make those Tourism Writing projects? Set up statewide tourism contests like the ones conducted by SELTI. Even private foundations can fund such projects when organized by nonprofit organizations or government agencies.

Finally, members of the media can produce interview features in their local, state, or national media related to the potential of tourism writing projects. If no local projects are currently ongoing to cover, then do a piece on whether or not such projects would benefit the area and on what types of attractions might be featured; there's plenty of reaction to be had on those types of stories, and when they run, it will inspire many local writers to pursue such projects in the near future. For example, reference similar projects in other states (like Alabama), and ask the mayor and local convention and visitor bureau director if he or she thinks the same type of writing might benefit the city or town. If you are a state reporter, ask the governor and state tourism direction the same question. If you are a national reporter for a major newspaper, radio, or television network, then interview national officials, up to the president and the cabinet, on the subject of tourism writing and how it could impact consumer spending through tourism dollars. With all of the economic media stories flowing into the market every day, a story with a new angle will generate extra attention and help it stand out in an innovative way.

Tourism Writing, as a genre, will be like any genre: the result of thousands of people's efforts, from writers to agents to publishers to booksellers to readers to reporters and countless others in the chain. There is a great deal of work involved, but there is also a great deal of fun! The only difference is, now the fun doesn't have to stop with the last page. Now the readers can experience the pages coming to life like never before.

Choosing a real place, using photos and links to other nearby points of interest, and directly inviting visitors encourages people to explore. As we say in the South, "Y'all come."

This type of writing is not done in a traditional form. It is neither an advertisement nor a travel guide. It is much more subtle. The place or event, photos, links, and special invitation are all woven into a short story, a novel, or even a poem. It requires research. You have to be accurate in your description of a place. You cannot have palm trees in woods full of oaks and pines. You cannot have sidewalks in the middle of a woodsy area where none exist. The photos you include in your story will show the difference. Not only that, but the first reader of your work may be familiar with the location. If that person spots an error, it is bad news. Once a reader discovers a discrepancy, he, or she, usually distrusts the rest of the writing. Being correct is a must.

When choosing a topic, try to think of a place or event unique to your area. Find something not many people know about, if possible. If you must choose a well-known site or event, attempt to put a new twist on it. Dig deep. See if you can find a special point of interest about it, a new angle that has not been explored previously. Tell the reader something they do not already know about the subject.

Next, make sure your style and tone are entertaining. Do not list and drone on. Use exciting phrases, active verbs, and descriptive adjectives that make things come to life. Help your readers connect with the issue or the characters. Get them emotionally involved. Then insert appropriate photos to illustrate your message and provide links to additional points of interest. Do not assume the reader considers himself, or herself, welcome. Give it a personal touch. At the end, issue your direct invitation to visit the area written about.

You can improve your writing by following some simple rules that apply to all creative writing. Here are a few of them:

THE OBVIOUS:

Use Spell Check, but don't trust it completely. It doesn't know the difference between the use of "their" and "there".

Have as many Beta readers as possible. Be sure to include an "average" person who reads for entertainment as one of them. Such a reader often catches plot errors academic people may miss. Listen to your critics. Don't take their criticism personally. It takes a tough skin to be a writer.

Make sure your diction isn't vague. Tell readers something they don't know. Be specific. Also, people like challenges. Many like to find words they need to look up to define.

Make sure your writing has CLOUT—coherence, logic, organization, unity and transition. Develop your story thoroughly, too, with good grabbers and cliffhangers.

Keep the tone and style consistent. Characters can change but they need a motive to do so. Choppy and stringy sentences can ruin a good story.

If you understand the characters and plot, so will your readers.

EDITORIAL PREFERENCES:
REMEMBER GOAL, MOTIVATION AND CONFLICT. MAKE THEM CLEAR.

Point of View—editors want writers to avoid head-hopping. Always stay in one character's head in a scene.

Show, don't tell. Action is better than words. BECOME your character. Write what he or she would do. Avoid words like saw, heard, felt, tasted, smelled, wondered, watched. Watch repeated words, phrases and sentences and keep words like "look" one to a page.

Facial expressions, body language and actions speak louder than adverbs; cut words ending in "ly". Also, use pronouns for proper names whenever it's clear who's speaking or acting. Search for "that" and words like "was" and you'll probably be surprised how many times they appear.

Before you submit, take the time to reread it for content and technical errors. Chances are you'll find something, or some things, everyone missed.

If you are seeking publication, study submission guidelines and follow them closely.

HAPPY WRITING AND BEST WISHES FOR SUCCESS

AFTERWORD

Why should we care about Tourism Writing? Tourism is a unique business. Traveling involves a lot more than how much a person can afford. It's not just about dollars and cents. People plan trips based on passion—how they feel about a place or event. It's an emotional decision that often involves sentiment. It also involves a desire to expand horizons by learning about something new, or a reminder of something experienced in the past, being recalled to it by strong memories, even though nobody can live a life backwards. But we can be cleansed. The past leads to the future and sometimes reliving an experience provides a catharsis that allows us to move forward.

Tourism Writing can show us the way. It can direct us to places and events by arousing our curiosity. When we read about either of those and see photos and links to them, we can make a connection, maybe one intense enough to take action, especially after seeing a direct invitation to visit and made to feel welcome. It's a new way to become intrigued and involved with the wide, wide world out there ready to open its doors to us.

If schools take up this cause and add Tourism Writing to their courses, chances are authors will soon include it in their books. Both established and new writers could profit from Tourism Writing. It could open doors with its wide range of possibilities, presenting a tempting challenge, a chance to use imagination in an unchained way. It offers an opportunity to see history in your own locality in a different light—a way to stand on historical spots and feel empathy for those who stood there in the past facing the unknown, experiencing the fear and the danger of the unexplored.

Hopefully, studying the genre and reading such writing will teach people how to lead a fuller life. Then the purpose of this book will be fulfilled.

BIBLIOGRAPHY

Allison, Neal, Floor Manager, Jelly Fish Restaurant, Perdido Key, FL, (2017, July 12. Personal Interview.

Barber, James, Executive Director of Public Safety, Mobile, AL, (2017, July 17). Personal Interview.

Battiste, Lawrence, Chief of Police, Mobile, AL, (2017, July 10). Personal Interview.

Beard, Chuck, East Side Story bookstore owner, Nashville, TN, (2017, July 29). Personal Interview.

Borom, John L., Ph.D, Coastal Alabama College Director, Fairhope, AL, President of Mobile Bay Audubon Society, (2017, September 21). E-mail Interview.

Bowers, Joyce, Mobile, AL Real Estate Agent, (2017, April 20). Telephone Interview.

Bradley, Vinson J., Director of Enrollment for Evening Studies, Huntingdon College, (2017, April 19). Personal Interview.

Bunn, Mike, director of capital expansion and public affairs, Blakeley Park, Mobile, AL, (2017, May 5). E-mail Interview.

Cink, Arnie, Former Dairy Farmer, Baldwin County, AL, (2017, September 3). Personal Interview.

Clark, David, President and CEO of Visit Mobile, (2017, May 18). Personal Interview.

Daniels, Margaret, retired teacher/coordinator in marketing and sales, (2017, April 20). Personal Interview.

Davis, Ben, Engineer (Retired), Fairhope, AL, (2017, April 25). E-mail Interview.

Day, James, Ph.D. History Professor, University of Montevallo, (2017, August 8). Telephone Interview.

Earnheart, Grady, Assistant Manager, I-10 Florida Welcome Center, (2017, July 12). Personal Interview.

Flowers, Ashley-Nicole Ross, Program Supervisor, MS, CTRS, City of Mobile Parks and Recreation, (2017, September 21). Personal Interview.

Fraiser, Judge Jim, Pass Christian, Harrison County, MS, author *The Majesty of Mobile*, (2017, April 22). Personal Interview.

Glassbrook, Daryn, Executive Director of the Mobile Medical Museum, (2017, May 13). Personal Interview.

Golson, Eva, Director of Mobile Film Office, (2017, August 9). Personal Interview.

Goodspeed, Hill, Historian, Naval Aviation Museum, Pensacola, FL, (2017, July 12). Personal Interview.

Green, Myrna, Hancock County, MS, Tourism Director, (2017, May 5). Personal Interview.

Green, Dr. Evelyn K., University of South Alabama Interim Chair of Hospitality and Tourism Management, (2017, September 12). Personal Interview.

Gurt, Deborah, Assistant Librarian and Digital Processing Archivist, McCall Rare Book and Manuscript Library, University of South Alabama, (2017, September 15). Personal Interview.

Hall, Diane, Assistant to Eva Golson at Mobile Film Office, (2017, August 09). Personal Interview.

Hamlin, Powell, Owner of Dew Drop Inn Restaurant, (2017, May 13). Personal Interview.

Jacob, Judith F., NFG USAF 164 MSG (Retired), Memphis, TN, (2017, July 18). E-mail Interview.

James, Bill, Owner of Kate Shepard House Bed and Breakfast, Mobile, AL, (2017, April 22). Personal Interview.

James, Wendy, Owner of Kate Shepard House Bed and Breakfast, Mobile, AL, (2017, April 22). Personal Interview.

Jones, Brian, media specialist for the Alabama Tourism Department, (2017, July 29). Personal Interview.

Kirby, Robert, Former President of the Better Business Bureau of South Alabama, (2017, April 30). Telephone Interview.

Lambert, Ron, Director of Marketing, Faulkner University, (2017, April 27). Personal Interview.

Levin, Dr. Philip, President of Gulf Coast Writers' Association, Emergency Room Physician, MS, (2017, April 22). Personal Interview.

Marston, Tighe, Manager of Magnolia Cemetery, (2017, July 10). Personal Interview.

McCoy, Sonny, Mobile Police Department corporal, (Retired) Driver for movie stars in Mobile, (2017, August 11). Telephone Interview.

McFayden, Meg, owner of Art and Invention Gallery, Nashville, TN, (2017, July 29). Personal Interview.

McKenzie, Jason, executive director of the Joe Jefferson Players, (2017, August 14). Personal Interview.

Montiel, David, Radiologist, Past President of the Medical Association of the State of Alabama, Past President of the Alabama Academy of Radiology Chapter of American College of Radiology, (2017, May 12). Personal Interview.

Morris, Kyle, Science Teacher, Cullman, AL, (2018, May 5). E-mail Interview.

Peterson, Karen, Senior Instructor, University of South Alabama, (2017, August 22). Personal Interview.

Pond, Ann, director of the Mobile Mardi Gras Trail, (2018, June 6). Personal Interview.

Richardson, Fred, Mobile City Councilman, Vice-President of District 1, (2017, June 15). Personal Interview.

Schluter, John, Lieutenant Colonel, USAF, (Retired) (2017, May 8). E-mail Interview.

Schneider, Gavin, Mobile History Museum, Tourism Department, Marketing and Events Coordinator, 2017, May 2). Personal Interview.

Smith, Wes, assistant manager of MoonPie Restaurant, Mobile, AL, (2017, June 24). Personal Interview.

Sparkman, Bill, Businessman in Nashville, TN and Mobile, AL, 7(2017, July 28). Personal Interview.

Tindle, Scott, co-owner of Colonial Fort of Mobile and Mobile Ducks, (2017, July 17). Personal Interview.

Torry, Chuck, Research Historian of the City of Mobile, (2017, May 2). Personal Interview.

White, Nolan, Assistant Editor of *Great Days Outdoors Magazine*, Spanish Fort, AL, (2017, July 5). Personal Interview.

Williams, George, Former Director of Tourism for the State of Alabama and the State of Maryland, (2017, May 5). Personal Interview.

Williams, Tish, Executive Director of the Hancock County Chamber of Commerce (MS) (2017, May 5). Personal Interview.

Woods, John O'Melveny, Intellect Publishing Company, Publisher (2017, April 21). Personal Interview.

Wright, Jason, metal artist, Laconia, Indiana, (2017, July 29). Personal Interview.

BOOKS

Marketing Places, Kotler, Philip, Haider, Donald H. Rein, Irving, The Free-Press A Division of Macmillan, New York, 1993 p. 44.

Pritchard, Andrew James, Naturalist, "The Man in Seat 11B".

MAGAZINES

Newton, Craig, *Great Days Outdoors Magazine*, February, 2014, page 9.

Powergrams, Alabama Power Co. magazine, January, February, 2017, *The French Connection*, Chuck Chandler, photography by Meg McKinney, p. 18.

Shipp, Bob, *Great Days Outdoors Magazine*, March 2013, page 46.

Steber, Tom, *Great Days Outdoors Magazine*, February, 2014, page 9.

NEWSPAPER ARTICLES

Mullen, John, Contributing Editor, "250—foot ship will become state's latest dive " – *Lagniappe Weekly* 8-3-17—8-9-1.

Ruddiman, Susan *The Mississippi Press*, February 10.

WEBSITES/INTERNET

www,cityofmobile.org/news.php?view=full&news-2778

www.mobile history museum.com

www.moonpiegeneralstore.om

www.magnoliacemetery.com

www.nam.com

CHMRSCC

www.laddpeeblesstadium.com

www.joejeffersonplayers.com

www.mobiletheaterguild.org

www.cctshows,com

www.playhouseinthepark.org

http://www.bbc.co.uk/guides/zg4dwmn#zc304wx

http://www.perfectbee.com/a-healthy-beehive/main-threats-to-bees

www.onlyinourstate.com/alabama/cheese-farm-al

www.EastSideStory.TN.com

www.artandinvention.com

gulfquest.org

https://www.npsgov/aboutus/history.htm: History of the National Park System.

Strauss, Dave, https://www.nature.org/aboutus/contact/index.htm Arlington, VA.

http://adsfr.com/about_rodeo

http://libmsstate.edu/grisham

https://www.southalabama.edu/colleges/ceps/htm

BiblioTech: Palfrey, John, Why Libraries Matter more than Ever in the Age of Google.

ABOUT THE AUTHOR

Mary S. Palmer is an accomplished, award-winning author who started writing when she was five years old. Her enthusiasm for the art never waned as is evident by her persistence in honing her craft by attending the University of South Alabama where she graduated Cum Laude with a Bachelor of Arts Degree, and she went on to obtain a Master of Arts Degree with a Concentration in Creative Writing.

She has had twelve books in different genres published, along with short stories, poems, essays, and two plays. Two of her books were published in the last year: *George Wallace: An Enigma*, a biography, and *Time Will Tell*, the first of a series of three science-fiction books. In 2014, her short story, *Raisin' Cain*, won the Southeastern Literary Tourism Initiative Award. It was presented to her by Congressman Bradley Byrne. *The Concrete Block Wall* won the Hackney Award in 2017.

She is also a lecturer in English at Faulkner University and a member of the adjunct faculties at Coastal Alabama College and Huntingdon College.

She loves to travel and has visited all fifty of the United States and every continent except Antarctica. She uses unusual incidents from those experiences in her books.